George M. Fairchild

Canadian Leaves

History, Art, Science, Literature, Commerce

George M. Fairchild

Canadian Leaves
History, Art, Science, Literature, Commerce

ISBN/EAN: 9783337186487

Printed in Europe, USA, Canada, Australia, Japan

Cover: Foto ©ninafisch / pixelio.de

More available books at **www.hansebooks.com**

Canadian Leaves

History, Art, Science, Literature, Commerce

A Series of New Papers

READ BEFORE THE

Canadian Club of New York

" Awake, my country, the hour of dreams is done !
Doubt not, nor dread, the greatness of thy fate."
ROBERTS.

EDITED BY
G. M. FAIRCHILD, JR.
Vice-Prés. C. C.

ILLUSTRATED BY
THOMSON WILLING
A. R. C. A.

NEW YORK
NAPOLÉON THOMPSON & CO., PUBLISHERS
51 AND 53 MAIDEN LANE

DEDICATED TO

HIS EXCELLENCY

THE MARQUIS OF LANSDOWNE

GOVERNOR GENERAL

of the

DOMINION OF CANADA

AS A TOKEN OF THE ESTEEM IN WHICH HE IS HELD BY THE
CANADIANS RESIDENT IN NEW YORK

PREFACE.

N apology is not needed in presenting this work to the Public, but one is due to the early subscribers for the delay in its appearance. A fire in the building occupied by the printers caused almost a total destruction of the printed sheets and necessitated a suspension of work for some time.

It is rare to find gathered into one volume so brilliant a series of original papers by so many distinguished authors and scientists. I feel a just pride that the pleasant task of editing them should have fallen to my lot. I have endeavored to give them a setting worthy of their value, and in this laudable effort I

viii   *Table of Contents.*

	PAGE.
The Mineral Resources of Canada, By John McDougall.	217
An Artist's Experience in the Canadian Rockies, By John A. Fraser, R. C. A.	233
Canada First, ... By Rev. George Grant, D. D., Principal Queen's University.	247
The Advantages of Commercial Union to Canada and the United States, . . . By Erastus Wiman.	269
The Canadian Club, ... By G. M. Fairchild, Jr.	283
Canadian Club Officers, 1887,	291

ERRATA.

Page 3, line 5, for *who seek*, read, which seek.
   " 108, line 23, for *guiding-hallow*, read, guiding-halo.
   " 113, " 15, for *introduced to court*, read, introduced at court.
Page 113, line 16, for *in waiting of*, read, in waiting to.
   " 115, " 20, for *laying*, read lying.
   " 141, " 25, transpose *Picturesque Canada* after *Ocean to Ocean.*

viii

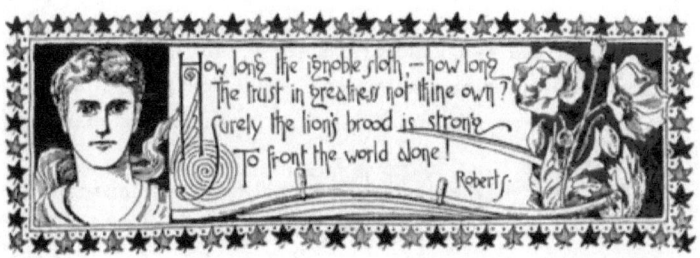

THE FUTURE OF THE DOMINION OF CANADA.

BY
EDMUND COLLINS.

{ An Address delivered before the
Canadian Club of New York.

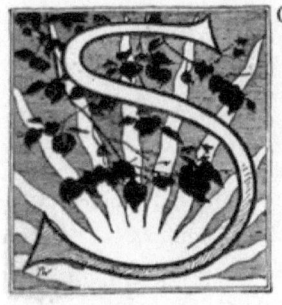OME of the greatest historians of the olden times, for the purpose of illustrating a nation's greatness, would only take into account the number of her spear's on the land, and of her galleys on the sea; and it must be confessed that, even in this age of industry and peace, we are not a little proud of our battalions and of the thunder of our turret guns.

In dealing with Canada, we have more substantial elements to fire our eloquence; we have her boundless acres, her limitless forests, and the exhaustless treasures of her mines and seas. Under the Confederation immense strides have been made in national development, and this I think ought to be a guarantee for the future.

But, after all, there are several gentlemen in Canada, who are not satisfied with the Union. Indeed, at very frequent intervals, some patriot who has failed in the pulpit or at the bar, who has brought a country school into disrepute, or added to the population of a graveyard, arises among his countrymen, and declares that the Confederation must be smashed. The intensity of his eloquence on such an occasion will be commensurate with his wants. If he is able to scrape along at all, he will not be very fierce, and will receive no great attention; but if there is neither brief, nor school, nor pulpit, nor consumptive in sight, he rises to the very highest pitch of patriotism, and some admiring organ of public opinion puts an "extra" at his disposal. If, in the experience of Dr. Johnson, "patriotism was the last refuge of a scoundrel," in ours, treason is the first refuge of a patriot.

I presume that those who hear me are not unaware that Nova Scotia has lately passed resolutions affirming a desire for separation, and there is a rumor in the air that New Brunswick wants to get adrift. I do not believe that these ideas will prevail; but they have undermined faith in the solidity of the Union, and Castle Garden receives the immigrant. It is no harm, however, to sin against the State. If you libel an individual, or decry his enterprise, the law will look after the matter; but assail the country whose institutions protect, and whose kindly breast sustains, and the Governor will select you as his chief adviser or his Secretary of State. For my part, instead of providing cabinet offices, I should prepare the cat and the pillory.

It may not be uninteresting, if not precisely cheerful, to enquire about the fate likely in store for the provinces who seek separation, in the event of the possibility of their release. In spite of the wealth which they boast of, to me they seem to stand up on the very verge of pauperdom. Enjoying the felicity of independence and isolation, each one would be a Lazarus at the gates of the Empire. We know very well that the expense of house-keeping, in Nova Scotia and in New Brunswick, is greater than either province is able to bear; and either one or the other is always found at Ottawa, with a threat or a prayer upon her lips, asking for still "better terms." Let us suppose one of these provinces cast adrift. Her only sources of income would be the proceeds from the sale and lease of her timber and mineral lands, and the toll of the custom-houses.

To-day Nova Scotia is almost completely stripped of her forest, and the area of woodland in New Brunswick is rapidly diminishing; and if there is but little income from the mines for the individual, there would be less for the public treasuries. The ship-yards are idle, and must remain so from now until the end of time; nor is there any industry in sight or in the distant future. Under the terms of confederation a sum of 80 cents per head is set apart from the Dominion treasury, and to hope that this amount could be made up under the régime of divorce, from the little provincial custom-houses, is mere delusion. For the lack of responsible guarantee, the obligations of these provinces would go begging in the money market. Capital and immigration would pass by their doors, and they would become the paupers of the Empire.

It is the custom, among certain people in the East, when famine afflicts the land, to enter the temples and belabor with clubs their favorite idols. As the timber becomes scarce, and revenue falls off, these good people by the sea wax fierce in their denunciation of taxes, as if the most weighty and unjustifiable tax of all, that on coal, were not merely maintained as a sop to them.

However, it may be said, once for all, that Nova Scotia and her sister will be saved from themselves. For there is no road leading out of the Union.

If, in discussing the prospects of Canada in general, I may be allowed to confine a few more observations to the maritime provinces, I should say that I believe their manifest local destiny to be maritime union. To superintend about a million and a half of public business, they have three petit kings, three houses of Commons, and at least two houses of Lords; while in number the judges and chief justices, to borrow a fantastic comparison, are as the stars of the heaven. But let alone the fact that each province requires a legislature, a governor, a cabinet and a standing army of officials, to transact half a million dollars of business, there must needs be in addition the pomp and circumstance of presenting arms, firing salutes and decking out in uniforms and cocked-hats.

I have heard many speeches delivered from those very provincial thrones at the opening of the legislature, and have noted some of their items. There is always a paragraph having reference to Providence and the harvests; and this seems to be quite fitting, for the harvests are about the only matter in their political economy in which the hand of Providence is to be seen. In New Brunswick, I once listened to one of those pretentious speeches from the throne wherein this passage occurred, the most important one of the whole communication : " During the year, my Government have given earnest attention to the affairs of the husbandman, and the improvement of stock ; and to this end have effected the importation of a superior breed of sheep." I turned to the itemized public accounts and found that the numerical strength of the importation consisted in six animals. Imagine putting on a cocked-hat and a sword to announce that a Government had brought in Canada six ewes and rams.

To sum up the matter, one capable business man could, without governor or cabinet, without volunteer or the firing of rusty cannon, effectually transact the whole affairs of the three petty provinces by the sea. I think, therefore, that the conclusion any sensible man would arrive at in this connection would be that these provinces ought and must rid themselves by fully one-half of their present expensive administration. This can be accomplished by a maritime union, which would give for the three provinces one lieutenant-governor, one legislature and but one army of official dependents instead of three.

An outsider listening to one of the maritime statesmen would assuredly hear him talk of retrenchments ; hear him cipher how much the Lieutenant-Governor squanders in paint and coal-oil, and naturally would ask himself why in thunder no mention is made of the larger items? He would scarcely hear a word about maritime union, because maritime union would be the death of fully one-third of the professional politicians. But, suppose this part of the difficulty removed, there would still be in the background the burning question : " Which province is to have the seat of government?" Nova Scotia would rather pay two dollars in civil expenditure, where only one is needed, than that " The Island," or New Brunswick should be able to say that she was the home of the government. It will be seen, therefore, that so long as the question remains in its present shape, the three pinched provinces will go on maintaining their overwhelming system of magnificence and expenditures.

There is, I think, one way out of the difficulty, and although I have elsewhere indicated the way, I may be permitted to once more refer to it. A few years ago, when a teacher made application for a school in a back district, the great difficulty in his way was the question of where to board. The thought that one settler should monopolize the honor and the profit of his domiciliation was in itself odious, and the matter was finally settled by his consenting to " board round the deestrict." Are we to infer from this, that if the government of these three little united provinces would consent to " board round the deestrict," the greatest obstacle to maritime union would be removed.

Before discussing the governmental alternatives left to Canada, we must preface our remarks by stating that the political atmosphere should first be made purer if we desire to contemplate with pride the future of the country. There are now in public life in Canada some good men; men who earnestly strive to use their talent for the general good : but, after all, such worthy ones are few. For the greater part, politics are in Canada what they are in the United States, one of the lowest of all the games that offer success to ability devoid of honor. The best men, and the most thoughtful among them in either country, are not to be found in political life; such men shrink from the ordeal which is the lot of the political candidate. The successful men are generally those who are popular in the billiard-room, liberal in treating at the bar, or foremost on the turf or lucky in the gambling pool. As a rule too, these men are without means and of no social standing; they are devoid also of education and of the knowledge indispensable to competently help in the making of laws. If a man enters public life without fortune and stripped of all honorable ambition, it is deadly certain that his chief aim is to further his own interests. Given an unscrupulous politician at the head of government, and he will buy these men as a butcher buys a flock of sheep.

It is true that these men give a semblance of patriotism to their movements by allying themselves with a party; but this party has become a machine, and the harm that the machine does to public interests and public morals is greater even than could be accomplished by loose fish who held themselves aloof from either side. I take it for granted that there is a splendid opportunity in store for young men in Canada, provided they stand aloof of the machines and take as their watchword, not Protection or Free-Trade, but the purification of public life. I say the young men, because the older ones have already suffered themselves to be bound to the wheel, and to the end will go sinning for the party rather than bring upon their brilliant names the reproach of "turncoat."

I affirm, without dread of refutation, that our country is worse now, and not better, for her politicians.

The Confederation is made up of interests more or less divergent, and of aims more or less conflicting; there is a slight antagonism of religion, and there is fierce conflict of races. The best and the noblest deed patriotism could perform would be to restore harmony to that part of the instrument which is jangled and out-of-tune; to seek and close up the joints in the Confederation; to demonstrate that the interest of the many ought to prevail over that of the few; that Canada is the country of the Gaul as well as of the Celt and the Saxon; and, finally, that the triumph of the country as a whole, in civilization and prosperity, is of far greater moment than the success or the aims of a section, a creed, or a race. Mr. Goldwin Smith describes the French province as a wedge driven between the Eastern and Western sections of the Union; but even this tenacious and exclusive nationality would in time blend into its surroundings if the politicians did not rekindle the old feuds periodically and were not continually unearthing for new discords. I do not think, however, that there is much room for anticipating that this province will readily submit to the logic of environment; if there were, such a hope dwindles down to mere nothingness when we find that the execution of a man convicted of treason and murder furnishing a new source of discord and isolation.

Before dismissing this chapter of my subject, I beg to point out one condition under which much could be done to improve political morals and draw men of character and fitness into public life. I think the honor of a seat in the legislature should be of itself a sufficient reward to the legislator. In England this is the rule, and instances like our own Pacific scandal, or the many frauds that blot political history in the United States is unheard of.

In our country, as in the States, a man imagines that an evil political deed brings no personal taint; until men are made to feel a reproach upon their public honor as keenly as a wound, the life of the legislator can not be an honest one, his calling an honorable calling. Honor is everything to most of the men who serve in Westminster, and for honor alone do they seek the place; their fortune puts them above the debasing influence money exercises, there we hear nothing of the sin so familiar to our own ears.

I am aware that it would be a grave injustice to the people of a young country to place its representation and its law-making power solely into the hands of those who could afford to serve without salary; for, at such a stage in a nation's life, every Cincinnatus handles his own plough. But the distribution of wealth is now wide enough to make the compensation one of honor; and wherever honor is the sole reward the best men only strives for the place. Admitting even that the twenty New York aldermen who perpetrated, in in the early morning, the foulest act known to municipal history, were not needy, we must concede on the other hand that they were the product of what is worst and dishonorable in the wards; if a higher standard of representation had obtained, candidatures as theirs would have been out of the question.

And now, I shall endeavor to briefly discuss the three alternatives which the future holds for Canada :—

First—Federation with the Empire.

Second—Annexation to the United States, and

Third—The formation of an independent nationality.

Federation is a vast scheme; nothing will so capture and dazzle a small mind as an omnipotent question. I may state, for the benefit of those who may have forgotten the fact, that the first public man of note in Canada to advocate Federation, was Sir Alexander Tilloch Galt;—but, looking over the files of old Canadian papers, I find that this same gentleman was at one time the leader of a movement in Montreal which sought to bring about annexation. But, such as the idea is, I have to deny credit for its origination with Sir Alexander, or for that matter with politicians. It was conceived by Mr. Justin McCarthy, who deals in some very splendid kite-flying in the closing portion of the history of Our Own Times. But Mr. McCarthy derived the inspiration from Tennyson, who, as everyone acquainted with *Locksley Hall* knows, tells us of a time when the war drum shall throb no longer,

> "And the battle flags be furled,
> In the parliament of man, the Federation of the World."

I wonder that somebody has not overtopped Lord Tennyson and taken in the moon. Sir John Macdonald, on account of whom I have been blamed for having over-praised him in my books, has latterly favored the idea: but Sir John is now nearly seventy-two, and a medical friend of mine, Dr. Ferguson, informs me, upon his professional reputation, that atrophy of the brain begins a little after fifty. Moreover, it must be remembered what influence an extra decoration, if it takes the form of a star or a pretty ribbon, has upon the understanding of men.

What puzzles me is how men like Sir John and Sir Alexander, so thorough in their examination of questions, and so sound in judgment, should have failed to find three or four objections to this project, any one of which is fatal. For instance, the fundamental notion in the scheme is the equality of the several portions of the Empire; but, if the existing Imperial constitution were to be preserved, this would mean colonial representation in the House of Lords as well as in the Commons. Colonial soil does not produce, that I am aware, peers of the realm; and the principle of entail and primogeniture is lacking to propagate the dignity and the status of a transplanted peerage. Imagine my grandson, the third Lord Collins of Canada, exercising his noble energies in sweeping chimneys!

Then, as to our concern in affairs of the Empire.

In the prestige and the power of Great Britain, we all glory, and the throbs of transport felt at the heart of the motherland thrills the colonists to the finger tips; but for all this we are not prepared to give our last man and our last shilling, as Sir George said we were; nor, for that matter, any man or any shilling, in erecting scientific frontiers, in making disastrous excursions through the Khyber pass, or shooting blacks in Ashantee. The British tax-payer may be persuaded that to bear the brunt of this class of undertaking is proper for him, because they maintain and augment the potency of the British name; but the Canadian tax-payer does not want, and will not bear, any share in such burdens. It would be only folly to expect otherwise, and this feature of the question is not worthy of further discussion.

Having disposed of these two barriers, let us picture to ourselves a contingent of representatives from Canada crossing the seas to discuss at Westminster whether a projected railroad bridge in Ontario should cross Swan's Creek or Duck's Puddle, and how much compensation deacon Estabrook's widow should receive for the slaughter of her cow or her husband by a government engine. Imagine the widow setting out from her farm to cross the wintry ocean in order to establish her claim before a listening England!

I suppose the question of divorce would be taken from the fond hands of the Ottawa senators to the House of Lords; and what a glorious occupation it would be for the Howards and the Stanleys to sit and hear the petition and the evidence of Martha Smith, and decide whether, after all, it was not best to turn the said Martha loose again into the matrimonial market.

Some one, among those present, will probably say that the Parliament of the Empire would have cognizance of only such questions as treaties, but three or four treaties in a life-time are about the number that past history has produced.

Let me repeat the fact that there is still a mightier question behind all this; it is found in the position that the heart of the Empire would occupy in relation to its outskirts. I am aware that our statesmen leave India out of the programme;

but, at the risk of repeating an old joke, I will affirm that this is like leaving Hamlet out of the play. Yet, even in doing this, I can, without danger of incurring the self-reproach of wildness, permit my imagination to travel to a time when the population of Canada alone will exceed that of the Imperial Island; so, when the representatives of goodly Canada would move into the house at Westminster, you would have the spectacle which Dundreary has best described, that of the tail waggling the dog.

Let those who smile remember that a federation on the mighty plan suggested is not a compact made for the span of a statesman's life, but a constitution fashioned to endure as long as the power and the glory of the British Empire last.

For these reasons and for a score of other good ones, I do not deem the scheme of federation to be either wise or practicable. It is a splendid subject to talk about, and, after all, it would be a pity to deny politicians the opportunity of discussing something grand now and again.

The second alternative is Annexation, and upon this I shall not waste many words. At the outset, allow me to remark that I can conceive of little in national ambition higher than a desire to form a portion of the mightiest Republic that the world has ever seen; but, with Canada, annexation would not mean alliance, it would simply mean absorption. Canadian individuality of course would cease, while the material condition of the people would not be improved. This, however, is a question about which we can only vaguely surmise. But I think that those who, like ourselves, have had an opportunity of comparing certain republican institutions with corresponding ones under English monarchy, can have no difficulty in giving the preference to those of the latter.

I shall not dwell upon the spectacle of the ermine trailed through the party mire and beholden to the bad men who pull caucus wires, for I should have to speak with some bitterness. I contend that the administration of justice in this country is not, nor can it be held above suspicion; for, it is not likely that the judge upon the bench can ignore the men who gave him his eminence; he would be more than human if he were able to forget those who can, at a stated time, give him that eminence again.

Nor would I, without a struggle, surrender the mild, I might say fictitious, kingly prerogative for that of the veto—which may be as arbitrary and capricious as the dictum of a Roman Emperor. If the veto is never arbitrary and never capricious, the man is to be thanked and not the constitution.

It would be well too, for those who contemplate the grandeur of a political brotherhood extending from the Isthmus of Panama to the land of the Esquimaux, to ponder whether or not there may not be somewhere a breaking point in national expansion.

Lastly, I do not think that our political vocabulary would gain much in elegance by the addition of such candidates as the "Mugwump" and the "Bloody Shirt."

But, whether there be any force or not in my objections, I think that I am not over bold in affirming that our people do not desire annexation and never will accept it.

Finally comes the proposal of national independence.

At the risk of shocking some of my hearers, I will state as

my belief that national independence is the more natural and logical future of Canada. I think it just as natural and just as logical that, in good time, the Dominion should end its connection with the cherished motherland, as it is for the boy, attaining man's estate, to leave his father's house and, single-handed, achieve his own fortune. But, come independence when it may, there will be no reddening of the land and no serious turmoil.

Mr. Gladstone stated his belief, less than three years ago, that if Canadians were to inform the mother country of their desire and readiness to stand alone, Great Britain would not say " No." After all, it will not be necessary to kill my friend Colonel Dennison or any of those U. E. Loyalists who carry the integrity of Canada upon the blade of their sword.

To put in a plea for Canadian independence, of course you are called upon to state the gains, and you are handed a bill of costs. Upon the list of gains I shall put first what some may count as nought, and that is sentiment: take sentiment out of the breast of man and he becomes a sordid grubber for his bread.

Independence would stimulate national ambition; it would give Canada a status in the eyes of the world, and divert immigration to her fertile lands.

Furthermore, it would give her the power to make and fashion treaties in accord with her commercial needs, and give her a place among nations.

Higher aims would prevail in the political sphere, and as a consequence ambition would be more lofty. In a word, it would give that for which some of the noblest men that ever lived, fought and bled and laid down their lives. I do not care to deal in heroics, but if the position of the guardian be higher than that of the ward, I take it that the standing of the independent state is superior to that of the dependent one. I do not see how there can be any dispute on this score.

Some will say: "Granted, but your independent Dominion will be a mere weakling among nations." And others may ask: "What can she do against hostile guns? What is to hinder the Republic at her side from swallowing her up?" I deny that she will be a weakling. Her population is greater now, and her defenses are stronger than were those of the American colonies at the time of their revolt. Her population is greater than any one of nearly a dozen independent European kingdoms, and she has a wider area of fertile land than any country on the face of the earth. Alone, the valley of the Saskatchewan, according to scientific computation, is capable of sustaining 800,000,000 souls. And along these boundless stretches of fertile wheat-land, herds and flocks live, without housing, through the winter season. In short, the capabilities of this country, about whose future the misinformed have doubts, are so great that an adequate recital of them would be simply amazing.

Let us now consider the dangers of an attack by hostile powers. In spite of all what pessimists may say, this is an age of peace and not of war; nations are not growing more warlike but more peaceful. We have reached at last the age of commerce, and to-day the battle is that of the ploughshare and not of the sabre. I do not think that we need fear to see any grapeshot sent across the Niagara, for our good friends the Americans are quite too busy making money to embark into such a profitless occupation. They have given us abundant proof that war is not upon their programme; for they maintain no mighty fleet nor grinding army, but only ships and muskets enough to serve as a police force on land and sea. Moreover, they remember that the Canadian volunteers knew how to fight as early as 1812, and they have not forgotten some of the lessons we taught them at Chrysler's farm, Châteauguay, and Queenston Heights.

Looking into the future, I perceive my country spanning this broad continent, her bosom throbbing with life and great plenty. Upon the pages of her history I can read the record of her achievements, it is worthy of a land with so rich an inheritance. I see her artists kneel for inspiration before her majestic and lovely landscapes, while able pens are moulding the traditions and legends with which the land is so richly strewn into an imperishable literature, encompassing history, romance and song.

Later on I imagine that I see a people—intelligent, thrifty and well-ordered—who, with roll of drum and the joyous waving of flags, celebrates the centennial anniversary of the birth of Canada; and I hear statesmen alluding to this nineteenth year of the Confederation, as the one which saw unworthy men strive to sever the ties of the sisterhood. Later on still, it seems as if I heard them relate with pride that in spite of these men's treason, the loyalty and faith of the people remained unshaken; that they went on adding and building, striving and achieving, until they crowned their work with a nationhood that in the eyes of civilized mankind stood second to none in prosperity, intelligence and general contentment.

18'

THE SCHISM IN THE ANGLO-SAXON RACE.

BY
GOLDWIN SMITH, M. A., D. C. L.

An Address delivered before the
Canadian Club of New York.

N the strength of the Anglo-Saxon race, —of which British institutions, now adopted by every European nation except Russia, the British Empire in India, and the American Republic, besides many a famous deed and glorious enterprise, are the proofs,— there lurks a weakness. It is the weakness of self-reliance pushed to an extreme, which breeds division and isolation. Races such as the Celtic race, weaker in the individual, are sometimes made by their clannish cohesiveness stronger in the mass. The

Celt seems to have lingered long in the clan state and to have had his character permanently moulded by it, while the Anglo-Saxon as a sea-rover came early out of that state and was trained from the infancy of the race to self-government. In enterprise and peril Anglo-Saxon will be the truest of comrades to Anglo-Saxon. But except under strong compression they are apt to fly apart. Even in travelling they hold aloof from each other. They quarrel easily and do not easily forget. Their pride perpetuates their estrangement. In their spleen and factiousness they take the part of outsiders against each other. It is thus that the race is in danger of losing its crown. It is thus that it is in danger of forfeiting the leadership of civilization to inferior but more gregarious races, to the detriment of civilization as well as to its own disparagement. The most signal and disastrous instance of this weakness is the schism in the race caused by the American Revolution with the long estrangement that has followed, concerning which I am to speak this evening.

You and I, gentlemen of the Canadian Club of New York; you, natives of Canada, and some of you perhaps descendants of United Empire Loyalists domiciled in the United States; I, an Englishman, holding a professorship of History in an American University—represent the Anglo-Saxon race as it was before the schism, as it will be when the schism is at an end. We remind the race of the time when its magnificent realm in both hemispheres was one, and teach it to look for the time when that realm will be united again, not by a political bond, which from the beginning was unnatural and undesirable, but by the bond of the heart. While the cannon of the Fourth of July are being fired, and the speeches are being made in honor of American Independence, we, though we rejoice in the birth of the American Republic, must toll the bell of mourning for the schism in the Anglo-Saxon race. We must ask ourselves, and so far as without offence we may exhort Americans to ask themselves, what the quarrel was about, whether it was such a quarrel as might reasonably breed, not only enmity for the time, but undying hatred; whether it ought not long before this to have given place to kinder and nobler thoughts; and whether by cherishing it and treating it as a point of national pride the Anglo-Saxon of the west does not disparage and traduce his own greatness.

The relation of political dependence between an Anglo-Saxon colony and its mother country was probably from the beginning unsound, and being unsound it was always fraught with the danger of a violent rupture. Perhaps it may be said that nothing could have averted such a rupture except a prescience which the wisest of statesmen seldom possess, or the teaching of a sad experience such as has led England since the American Revolution to concede to Canada and her other colonies virtual independence. The Greek colonist took the sacred fire from the altar hearth of the parent state and went forth to found a greater Greece in perfect independence, owing the parent state no political allegiance but only filial affection. It might have been better if the Anglo-Saxon, fully the equal of the Greek in colonizing faculty and power of political organization, had done the same. In this way it was that England herself had been founded. But the sentiment of personal allegiance to the Sovereign in whose realm the emigrant had been born was strong in all feudal communities. It shows itself clearly in the covenant made on landing by the emigrants of the *Mayflower*, nor had it by any means lost its hold over the minds even of men who took part in the American Revolution. In the period during which the colonies were founded this sentiment was universal. The colonies of the United Netherlands were dependencies as well as those of the Spanish, French, and British monarchies. They were dependencies, and as such they were protected and supported by the military power of the parent state. Had the British colonies not been protected and supported by the arms of England, would this continent have become the heritage of the English-speaking race? The English colonist was stronger no doubt than the colonist of New France; but was he stronger than the colonist of New France backed by the French fleets and armies? Might he not, instead of calling this vast and peerless realm his own, have merely shared it with three or four other races between whom and him there would have been a balance of power, rivalry, war and all the evils from which afflicted and over-burdened Europe sometimes dreams of escaping by means of a European Federation? Might he not even have entirely succumbed to the concentrated power of the French monarchy, wielded by the strong hand and the towering ambition of a Richelieu or a Louvois? These are contingencies unfulfilled, but unfulfilled perhaps because one memorable morning, on the Heights of Abraham, a British army and a British hero decided that Anglo-Saxon, not French, should be the language; that Anglo-Saxon, not French, should be the polity and the laws of the New World. And when that day was won there burst from the united heart of the whole race in both hemispheres a cheer not only of triumph but of mutual affection and of Anglo-Saxon patriotism which history still hears amidst the cannon of the Fourth of July.

Was the connection felt by the colonists to be generally oppressive and odious, or was the cause of quarrel merely a dispute on a particular point with the home government of the day? In the first case it might be natural, if not reasonable or noble, to cherish the feud; in the second, it clearly would be unnatural. That the connection was not felt to be oppressive and odious, but, on the contrary, to the mass of the colonists was dear and cherished, is a fact of which, if all the proofs were produced, they would more than fill my allotted hour. Franklin said, only a few days before Lexington, that he had more than once travelled almost from one end of the continent to the other, and kept a variety of company eating, drinking, and conversing with them freely, and never had heard in any conversation from any person, drunk or sober, the least expression of a wish for separation or hint that such a thing would be advantageous to America. Jay said, that before the second petition of Congress, in 1775, he never heard an American of any class or of any description express a wish for the independence of the colonies. Jefferson said, that before the commencement of hostilities he had never heard a whisper of a disposition to separate from Great Britain, and after that the possibility was contemplated by all as an affliction. The Fairfax County "Resolves" denounce as a malevolent falsehood the notion breathed by the Minister into the ear of the King that the colonies intended to set up for independent States. Washington, on assuming the command, declared, in his reply to an address from New York, that the object of the war was a restoration of the connection on a just and constitutional footing. Madison, at a later day, avowed that it had always been his impression that a re-establishment of the colonial relations to the parent country, as they were previous to the controversy, was the real object of every class of the people till the hope of obtaining it had fled. Dickinson was not more opposed to arbitrary taxation than he was to separation, and the fiery Otis might be called as a witness on the same side.* Men there were no doubt, like Samuel Adams, republicans in sentiment and devoted to political agitation, who from the beginning aspired to independence and meant to bring about a rupture; but they found it necessary to cloak their designs, and that necessity was the proof that the general sentiment was in favor of the connection.

There is another proof of the same fact which is familiar to every Canadian mind and of which Canada herself is the lasting embodiment. It is found in the number and constancy of the Loyalists whose annals have been written in a most generous spirit by a representative of their enemies, Mr. Sabine, and whose illustrious and touching heritage of misfortune is still the light and pride of not a few Canadian hearths in the land in which, by the insensate cruelty of the victor, the vanquished were compelled to seek a home. There seems reason to believe that fully one-half of the people, including a fair share of intelligence, remained at least passively

---

* I owe most of these citations to Mr. Sabine.

loyal till the blundering arrogance and violence of the royal officers estranged multitudes from the royal cause. Twenty-five thousand Americans, as Sabine thinks, according to the lowest computation, were in arms for the crown. To the end there were whole batallions of them serving in the royal army. Sabine says that Sir Guy Carleton sent away twelve thousand exiles for loyalty's sake from New York before the evacuation. Judge Jones, in the history the publication of which we owe to the New York Historical Society, gives a much larger number. Two thousand took their departure even from the shores of Republican Massachusetts. When the Netherlands cast off the yoke of Spain, when Italy cast off the yoke of Austria, how many Dutchmen or Italians went into exile out of loyalty to the oppressor?

This was not like the revolt of the Netherlands or of Italy, a rising against a foreign yoke: it was a civil war, which divided England as well as the United States. The American party in the British Parliament crippled the operations of the government and upon the first reverses enforced peace. Otherwise the loss of Cornwallis's little army would not have been the end. The contest would have been carried on by Great Britain with the same unyielding spirit which, after a struggle of twenty years, overthrew Napoleon.

"It is the glory of England," says Bancroft, "that the rightfulness of the Stamp Act was in England itself the subject of dispute. It could have been so nowhere else. The King of France taxed the French colonies as a matter of course; the King of Spain collected a revenue by his will in Mexico and Peru, in Cuba and Porto Rico, and wherever he ruled. The

States-General of the Netherlands had no constitutional scruples about imposing duties on their outlying possessions. To England exclusively belongs the honor that between her and her colonies the question of right could arise; it is still more to her glory, as well as to her happiness and freedom, that in that contest her success was not possible. Her principles, her traditions, her liberty, forbade that arbitrary rule should become her characteristic. The shaft aimed at her new colonial policy was tipped with a feather from her own wing." The reason why the colonies took arms, in short, was not that they were worse treated by their mother country than other colonists in those days, but that they were better treated. They rebelled not because they were enslaved, but because they were so free that the slightest curtailment of freedom seemed to them slavery. Whig and Tory, as Mr. Sabine says, wanted the same thing. Both wanted the liberty which they had enjoyed; but the Whig required securities while the Tory did not. The Tory might have said that he had the securities which Bancroft himself has enumerated, those afforded by the traditions, the Constitution, the political spirit of England herself, against any serious or permanent aggression on colonial liberty; and that while he possessed, in municipal self-government, in jury trial, in freedom of conscience and of the press, in the security of person and of private property, the substance of freedom, he would exercise a little patience and try whether the repeal of the Tea Duty could not be obtained before he plunged the country into civil war. The Stamp Duty had been repealed, and though at the same time the abstract right of parliament to tax the colonies had been asserted, this had been done with the full concurrence of Burke, and manifestly by way of saving the dignity of the Imperial legislature. The Tea Duty, trifling in itself, was a mere freak of Townsend's tipsy genius, to which the next turn in the war of parliamentary parties might have put an end, if colonial violence had not given a fatal advantage to the party of violence in the Imperial government. Nor does it seem to have been clear from the outset, even to the mind of Franklin, that the Imperial Parliament, had not the legal power of taxing the colonies, unwise and unjust as the exercise of that power might be. It was the only Parliament of the Empire, and in regard to taxation as well as other matters, in it or nowhere was sovereign power. That it had absolute power of legislation on general subjects, including trade, was admitted on all hands; and surely the distinction is fine between the power of general legislation and a power of passing a law requiring a tax to be paid. That there should be no taxation without representation might be a sound principle, but in the days of the unreformed Parliament it did not prevail in the mother country herself. Ship-money, to which the Tea Duty has been compared, was part of a great scheme of arbitrary government. It was intended, together with other devices of fiscal extortion, to supply the revenue for an unparliamentary monarchy, the reactionary policy of which in Church and State would, in Hampden's opinion, have quenched not only the political freedom but the spiritual life of the nation, and made England the counterpart and the partner in reaction of France and Spain. Nothing like this could be said of the Tea Duty. Bancroft acquits Grenville of any design to introduce despotism into the colonies. Such a design could hardly have entered the mind of a Whig who was doing his best to reduce to a nullity the power of the King. What Grenville desired to introduce was contribution to Imperial armaments, and he may at least be credited with the statesmanship which regarded the colonies, not as a mere group of detached settlements, but as an English Empire in the New World. The King may have had absolutist notions with regard to colonial as well as to home government, but the King was not an autocrat. The bishops may have wished to introduce the mitre, but the bishops were not masters of Parliament. Chatham was more powerful than King or bishops, and had his sun broken for an hour through the clouds which had gathered round its setting, the policy of the home government towards the colonies would at once have been changed.

The preamble of the Declaration of Independence sets forth a series of acts of tyrannical violence committed by George III., and it suggests that these were ordinary and characteristic acts of the King's government. Had they been ordinary and characteristic acts of the King's government they would have justified rebellion; but they were nothing of the kind. They were measures of repression, ill-advised, precipitate and excessive, but still measures of repression, not adopted before violent resistance on the part of the colonists had commenced. No government will suffer its officers to be outraged for obeying its commands and their houses to be wrecked, or the property of merchants trading under its flag to be thrown into the sea by mobs. Jefferson, who penned the Declaration, is the object of veneration to many, but his admirers will hardly pretend that he never preferred effect to truth.

One count in Jefferson's draft of the Declaration he was obliged to withdraw. In inflated, not to say fustian phrase, and with extravagant unfairness, he charges George III., who, though he had a narrow mind, had at least as good a heart as Jefferson himself, with having been specially to blame for the existence of slavery and of the slave trade. "He has waged," it says, "cruel war against human nature, violating its most sacred rights of life and liberty in the persons of a distant people who never offended him, captivating and carrying them into slavery in another hemisphere or to incur miserable death in their transportation thither. This piratical warfare, the opprobium of infidel powers, is the war of the Christian King of Great Britain. Determined to keep open a market where men should be bought and sold, he has prostituted his negative for suppressing any legislative attempt to prohibit or restrain this execrable commerce." This count, as we know, was struck out in deference to the sentiments of patriots, heirs of the spirit of Brutus and Cassius, who were perpetuating and were resolved, if they could, to go on perpetuating the violation of sacred rights and the piratical warfare laid to the charge of George III. Not the least curious, surely, of historical documents is this manifesto of a civil war levied to vindicate the sacred principle that all men are born equal and with inalienable rights to liberty and happiness, when we consider that not only was the manifesto framed by a slave-owner and signed by slave-owners, but the Constitution to which the victory of the principle in the war gave birth embodied a fugitive-slave law and a legalization of the slave trade for twenty years.] A stranger inducement surely never was held out to men to fight in the cause of human freedom than that which was offered by Virginia to volunteers, three hundred acres of land and one sound and healthy negro. Equity compels us to admit that the want of a thorough grasp of the principle of liberty was not limited to the mind of George III. A Virginian planter fought not for freedom, the love of which had never entered his soul: he fought for his own proud immunity from control and for the subjection to his will of all around him. His haughtiness could hardly brook even association with the mercantile and plebeian New Englander in military command. Suppose the negro had taken arms in vindication of the principle that all men were born equal and with an inalienable right to liberty and happiness, his manifesto would have been tainted by no fallacy like that which taints the Declaration of Independence. The acts of tyranny and cruelty of which he would have complained, the traffic in human flesh, the confiscation of the laborer's earnings, the chain and the lash, the systematic degradation of the slave, and all the wrongs of slavery, would have been not temporary measures of repression, adopted by authority in self-defence; they would have been normal and characteristic of the system.

On Jefferson's principle of framing indictments against governments what an indictment might the Loyalists again have framed against the government of Independence! "We have adhered," they might have said, "to a connection dear to all of you but yesterday, to the allegiance in which we were born, to a form of government which seems the best to us, and not to us only, but to Hamilton and others of your leading men, who avow that if Constitutional monarchy were here attainable they would introduce it here. For this we have been ostracized, insulted, outraged, tortured, pillaged, hunted down like wild beasts. The amnesty which ought to close all civil wars has been denied us; some of us have been hanged before the face of our departing friends; and now we are stripped of all our property and banished from our native land under threat of death if we return. Even women, who cannot have borne arms in the royal cause, if they have property, are included in the proscription and in the sentence of death. The proscription list shows, too, that membership of the Church of England is practically treated as a crime!" Surely these complaints would have been not less pertinent than those of Jefferson against George III. Atrocities had no doubt been committed by the Loyalists, but, as Mr. Sabine says, they had been committed on both sides. Conscientious error is no crime in politics any more than in religion, though it is treated as a crime by fanatical revolutionists as well as by inquisitors.

Supposing even the Loyalists could have foreseen the present success of the American Republic, and with the success the evils and dangers which disquiet thoughtful Americans, would they have been very base or guilty in shrinking from revolution? We are on the Pisgah of Democracy, but not yet in the promised land. No one is in the promised land at least, except Mr. Carnegie who, in his genial and jocund hymn of triumph, pouring forth his joyous notes like a sky-lark of democracy poised over the caucus and the spoils system, ascribes it to Democratic institutions that the Mississippi is as large as twenty-seven Seines, nine Rhones, or eighty Tibers. The Democracy which shall make government the organ of public reason, and not of popular passion or of the demagogism which trades upon it, is yet in the womb of the future. Canada exults in having exchanged her royal governors for a government which is called responsible, though nothing is less responsible than a dominant party. In time, we trust, her exultation will be justified; but there is too much reason to doubt whether the rule of an honorable and upright gentleman, trained not in the vote-market but in the school of duty, such as General Simcoe or Sir Guy Carleton, was not, politically as well as morally, better for all but professional politicians, than a reign of faction, demagogism and corruption. Forwards not backwards we must look, forwards not backwards we must go. Yet history may extend its charity to those who, when they were not smarting under intolerable or hopeless oppression, shrank from passing through a Red Sea of civil bloodshed to a Canaan which was beyond their ken.

Besides the Tea Tax, no doubt, there were the restrictions on trade. These were in reality a more serious grievance, and probably they had at bottom at least as much to do with the Revolution as the Tea Tax. But such were the economical creed and the universal practice of the day. Chatham, the idol of the colonists, it was who threatened that he would not allow them to manufacture a horse-nail. The colonists themselves probably, though they groaned under restrictions, shared the delusion as to the principle in pursuance of which the restrictions were imposed, and they enjoyed privileges granted on the same principle and equally irrational which were supposed to be a compensation. The light of economical science had then barely dawned. Even now the shadows of the restrictive policy linger in the valleys though the peaks have caught the rays of morning.

There were Americans who desired a Republic. Samuel Adams we can hardly doubt was one of them. Judge Jones tells us that there was a Republican association at New York with classical phrases and aspirations. The patriotism of those days, the patriotism of Wilkes and Junius, was classical, not religious, like that of Hampden and Cromwell. It affected the Roman in everything, and was not unconnected with Roman Punch. But had George III. offered his colonial subjects a Republic, his offer would have been rejected by an overwhelming majority. Jefferson was a Rousseauist and a French revolutionist in advance. When Jacobinism came on the scene his affinity to it appeared. He palliates, to say the least, the September massacres and gives his admirers reason for rejoicing that he was not a Parisian, since, if he had been, he might have canted with Robespierre and murdered with Billaud Varennes. " My own affections," he says, " have been deeply wounded by some of the martyrs to this cause, but rather than it should have failed I would have seen the earth desolated. Were there but an Adam and Eve kept in every country and left free it would have been better than it now is." So inestimable to this slave-holder appeared the boon of liberty, even the liberty of a bedlam turned into a slaughter-house, even the liberty which went yelling about the streets with the head of a Farmer-General or the fragments of a Court lady's body on a pole. Jefferson and his fellow Jacobins had not learned what the Puritans of the English Revolution had learned, that you cannot, merely by getting rid of kings, make the soul worthy to be free. They had not learned that tyranny is the offspring, not of monarchy, but of lawless passion in the possessors of power, and that it can wear the Jacobin's cap-of-liberty as well as the despot's crown. A true brother of Rousseau who preached domestic reform and sent his own children to the foundling hospital, Jefferson declaimed against slavery and kept his slaves. His theories may have been true and his sentiments may have been beautiful, but the British government could not have been reasonably expected to shape its colonial policy so as to satisfy a Rousseauist and a Jacobin. Hamilton, as I have said, avowed his belief that constitutional monarchy was the best of all forms of government. He thought the House of Lords an excellent institution. Mason said that to refer the choice of a proper character for a chief-magistrate to the people would be like referring a trial of colors to a blind man. Betwen the sentiments of these men and Jefferson's democracy the difference was as wide as possible. It would have been difficult for poor George III. to satisfy them all.

It is unquestionably true that the conquest of French Canada, by setting the British colonists free from the fear of French aggression and rendering the protection of the mother country no longer necessary to them, opened the door for their revolt. But this, again, to say the least, is no proof that the colonies had been oppressed by the mother country. Had she left the French power on this continent unassailed in order that it might bridle them, her councils might have been reasonably branded with Machiavelism and bad faith.

The ostensible cause of this civil war, of the schism in our race and the violent rending of its realm, must be confessed, I submit, to have been inadequate. In their hearts the people felt it to be so, and their feeling showed itself, I cannot help thinking, in the languid prosecution of the war on the revolutionary side. States fail to send their contingents or their contributions, the armies are always melting away, brave men leave the camp on the eve of battle, the Federal cause is served without enthusiasm; only the local resistance, where the people were fighting for their homes as well as on their own ground, is really strong. Better materials for soldiers never existed, and the colonies must have set out with many thousands of men trained in colonial or Indian wars. The royal armies were about the worst ever sent out from England, and every possible blunder, both military and moral, was committed by the royal generals, who allowed advantages to slip from their hands which Wolfe or Clive would certainly have made fatal while they estranged multitudes of waverers who were inclined to return to their allegiance. Yet Washington's last words before the arrival of succor from France are the utterance of blank despair. "Be assured," he writes to Laurens, the agent in France, in April, 1771, "that day does not follow night more certainly than it brings with it some additional proof of the impracticability of carrying on the war without the aid you were directed to solicit."

Nor is it only of want of zeal and vigor that Washington and those who shared his responsibility complain; they complain, and complain most bitterly, of self-seeking, of knavery, of corruption, of monopoly and regrating, heartlessly practised in the direst season of public need, of murderers of the cause who were building their greatness on their country's ruin. They complain that stock-jobbing, peculation, and an insatiable thirst for riches, have got the better of every other consideration in almost every order of men, and that there is a general decay both of public and of private virtue. In order that contractors may fatten, armies go unfed and unclothed, tracing the line of their winter march with blood from their shoeless feet. Congress pays its debts with paper which it tries, like the French Jacobins, to force into circulation by penal enactment, and which, like the French assignats, opens an abyss of robbery, breach of contract and gambling speculation, an abyss so foul that Tom Paine himself afterwards proposed that whoever suggested a return to paper money should be punished with death. Washington's indignant hand lifts a corner of the veil of secrecy which covered the proceedings of Congress and the life of its members at Philadelphia. There was at least as much public spirit among these people as there was among any other people in the world. But the cause had not been sufficient to call it forth. As soon as the tar barrels of revolutionary excitement had burned out, the enthusiasm of the Sons of Liberty failed. The insurgents of the Netherlands, when they struggled onwards through wave after wave of blood to independence, had behind them the hell of Spanish rule. The American insurgents had behind them no hell, but a connection in which they had enjoyed the substantial benefits of freedom; and, after tasting civil war, most of them probably wished that things could only be as they had been before.

The relation between a dependent colony and the imperial

country, I repeat, was probably from the beginning false. At all events separation was inevitable; it was impossible that the Anglo-Saxon realm in both hemispheres should remain forever under one government, when the hour of political maturity for the colonies had arrived, especially as there was a certain difference of political character between the Anglo-Saxon of the old country and the Colonist which prevented the same policy from being equally suitable to both. What is to be deplored, if any foresight or statesmanship could have prevented it, is the violent rupture. What was to be desired, if human wisdom with the lights which men then possessed could have achieved it, was that the two portions of our race should have divided its realm in peace. Shelburne and Pitt seem to have wished and tried, when the struggle was over, to get back into something like an amicable partition of the Empire. Among other happy effects of such a settlement the fisheries' dispute would have been avoided. But the wound was too deep and too fresh. Shelburne and Pitt failed, and the two great Anglo-Saxon realms became absolutely foreign countries—unhappily, they became for many a day worse than foreign countries—to each other. Suppose, however, that not only the separation but the rupture was inevitable; because the inevitable came to pass, were the two branches of the race to be enemies forever?

Let the Fourth of July orator ask himself what were the consequences to England, to America, to the French monarchy, which, out of enmity to England, lent its aid to American revolution, and to mankind. To England the consequences were loss of money, which she could pretty well afford, and of prestige which she soon repaired. The Count de Grasse, as the monument at Yorktown records, received the surrender of Cornwallis who, hemmed in by three or four times his effective number, could get no fair battle and was taken like a wounded lion pent up in his lair. But Rodney who did get fair battle did not surrender to the Count de Grasse. Spain, too, must needs interfere in the Anglo-Saxon quarrel; but on the blood-stained and flame-lighted waters of Gibraltar sank the last armament of Spain; and the day was not far distant when she was to invoke the aid of England as a redeemer from French conquest. England went into the fight with Napoleon, for the independence of Europe, as powerful and indomitable as she had gone into the fight with Philip II. or with Louis XIV. Her great loss was that of the political enlightenment which she might have received from an experiment in democracy tried by a kindred people at her side, while her politics have perhaps been somewhat deflected from the right line of development by the repellant influence of galling memories and of friction with an unfriendly Republic. The colonies having been the scene of war must have lost more men and money than England, besides the banishment, when the war had closed, of no small number of their citizens. This loss they soon repaired, but they also lost their history and that connection with the experiences and the grandeurs of the past which at once steadies and exalts a nation. What was worse than this, the Republic was launched with a revolutionary bias which was the last thing that it needed. At the same time there was engendered a belief in the right of rebellion and in the duty of sympathizing with it on all occasions, which was destined to bear bitter fruit at last. The rebellion of the South in 1861 was manifestly inspired by sentiments nursed and consecrated by the Revolution. I remember seeing some words of Abraham Lincoln, in his earlier days, on the right of rebelling as often as people were dissatisfied with their government, which it seemed to me would have justified Southern secession.

Another consequence was the schism of the race on this continent, issuing in the foundation of a separate and hostile Canada, which, in the course of a few years, was to encounter the Revolutionary colonies in arms and to defend itself against them with at least as much energy and as much success as they had defended themselves against England. British emigration, moreover, was diverted from America to Australia; Anglo-Saxon cities which might have grown up here grew up on the other side of the globe; and the Anglo-Saxon element on this continent, in which the tradition and faculty of self-government reside, was thus deprived of a re-inforcement the loss of which is felt when that element has to grapple with a vast influx of foreign emigration untrained in self-government.

To the French monarchy the consequence was bankruptcy, which drew with it utter ruin, and sent the King to the scaffold, and Lafayette to an Austrian prison. To humanity the consequence was the French Revolution, brought on by the bankruptcy of the French monarchy and by the spirit of violent insurrection transmitted from America to France. Of all the calamities which have ever befallen the human race the French Revolution, as it seems to me, is the greatest. If any one is startled by that assertion let him review the history of the preceding half century, see what progress enlightenment had made, and to what an extent liberal and humane principles had gained a hold upon the governments of Europe. Let him consider how much had been done or was about to be done in the way of reform by Turgot, Pombal, Aranda, Tanucci, Leopold of Tuscany, Joseph of Austria, Frederic, Catherine, and Pitt. The American Revolution brought the peaceful march of progress to a violent crisis. Then followed the catastrophe in France, the Reign of Terror, the military despotism of Napoleon, the Napoleonic wars, desolating half the world and lending ten-fold intensity to the barbarous lust of bloodshed, the despotic reaction of 1815, another series of violent revolutions, another military despotism in France, with more wars in its train; and, on the other hand, Communism, Intransigentism, and all the fell brood of revolutionary chimeras to which Jacobinism gave birth, and which, imported into this continent by political exiles, are beginning to breed serious trouble even here. Separation, once more, was inevitable; but if it could only have been peaceful what a page of calamity, crime, and horror, would have been torn from the book of fate!

Then came the disastrous and almost insane war of 1812, an after-clap of the war of the Revolution. So far as that war was on the American side a war for the freedom of the seas it was righteous. Nobody can defend the Orders in Council, or the conduct of the British government, and the only excuse is that Great Britain was then in the agony of a desperate struggle, not for her own independence only, but for the independence of all nations. So far as it was a war of anti-British feeling and of sympathy with Jacobinism, as to a great extent it was, the protest of Webster and New England, it appears to me, may be sustained. That strife over and its bitterness somewhat allayed, there came disputes respecting the boundaries of Canada and at the same time bickerings about the slave trade, which England was laboring with perfect sincerity to put down. Later still came the quarrel bred by the sympathy of a party in England with Southern secession. I saw something of that controversy in my own country, standing by the side of John Bright against the dismemberment of the great Anglo-Saxon community of the West, as I now stand by the side of John Bright against the dismemberment of the great Anglo-Saxon community of the East. The aristocracy of England as a class was naturally on the side of the Planter aristocracy of the South, as the Planter aristocracy of the South would, in a like case, have been on the side of the aristocracy of England. The mass of the nation was on the side of freedom, and its attitude effectually prevented not only the success but the initiation of any movement in Parliament for the support or recognition of the South. If some who were not aristocrats or Tories failed to understand the issue between the North and the South, and were thus misguided in the bestowal of their sympathies, let it in equity be remembered that Congress, when the gulf of disunion yawned before it, had shown itself ready not only to compromise with slavery, but to give slavery further securities, if, by so doing, it could preserve the Union. Not a few friends of the Republic in England stifled their sympathy because they deemed the contest hopeless and thought that to encourage perseverance in it was to lure the Republic to her ruin. When

Mr. Gladstone proclaimed that the cause of disunion had triumphed and that Jeff. Davis had made the South a nation, some there were who echoed his words with delight ; not a few there were who echoed them in despair. I first visited America during the civil war, when the Alabama controversy was raging in its full virulence. Even then I was able to write to my friends in England that, angry as the Americans were, and bitter as were their utterances against us, a feeling towards the old country, which was not bitterness, still had its place in their hearts ; and it seems not chimerical to hope that the feeling which was thus shown to be the most deeply seated will in the end entirely prevail. In England, already, a display of the American flag excites none but kindly feelings, and the time must surely come when a display of the flag which American and British hands together planted on the captured ramparts of Louisburg will excite none but kindly feelings here.

The political feud between the two branches of the race would now I suppose be nearly at an end, if it were not for the Irish, or rather for the Irish vote. I am not going into the question of Home Rule, or as it would more properly be called, the question of Celtic secession. But I wish to impress upon my hearers one fact, which, unless it can be denied or its plain significance can be rebutted, is decisive, as it seems to me, of the Irish question. The north of Ireland is not more favored by nature than other parts ; its laws, its institutions, its connection with Great Britain under the Union, are precisely the same as those of the other provinces ; the only difference is that, having been settled by the Scotch, it is mainly Anglo-Saxon and Protestant, while the rest of the Island is

Celtic and Catholic; and the north is prosperous, contented, law-abiding and loyal to the Union. This fact, I say, appears to me decisive, nor have I ever seen an attempt on the part of secessionists to deal with it or rebut the inference. To extend Anglo-Saxon constitutionalism and legality to the clannish and lawless Celt, who after the Anglo-Saxon settlement in England still had his abode in Cornwall, Wales, the Highlands of Scotland, and Ireland has been a hard and tedious task. Cornwall was Anglo-Saxonized early, though traces of the Celtic temper in politics still remain. Wales was Anglo-Saxonized later by Edward the First, and the Kings his successors, who perfected his work. The Highlands of Scotland were not Anglo-Saxonized till 1745, when the last rising of the Clans for the Pretender was put down, and law, order, settled industry, and the Presbyterian Church penetrated the Highland glens with the standards of the United Kingdom. The struggle to make the Celtic clans of Ireland an integral and harmonious part of the Anglo-Saxon realm, carried on from age to age amidst untoward and baffling influences of all kinds, especially those of the religious wars of the Reformation, form one of the most disastrous and the saddest episodes of history; though it must be remembered that struggles not unlike this have been going on in other parts of Europe where national unification was in progress, without receiving so much critical attention or making so much noise in the world. One great man was for a moment on the point of accomplishing the work and stanching forever the source of tears and blood. That Cromwell intended to extirpate the Irish people is a preposterous calumny. To no man was extirpation less congenial; but he did intend to make an end of Irishry, with its clannishness, lawlessness, superstition, and thriftlessness, and to introduce the order, legality, and settled industry of the Anglo-Saxon in its place. To use his own expression he meant to make Ireland another England, as prosperous, peaceful, and contented. It is impossible that British statesmen can allow a separate realm of Celtic lawlessness to be set up in the midst of the Anglo-Saxon realm of law; if they did, the consequence would be civil war, murderous as before, between the two races and religions in Ireland, then reconquest and a renewal of the whole cycle of disasters. Nor can any government suffer the lives, property, and industry of its law-abiding citizens to be at the mercy of a murderous conspiracy, or permit terrorism to usurp the place of the law. Butchering men before the faces of their wives and families, beating out a boy's brains in his mother's presence, setting fire to houses in which men are sleeping, shooting or pitch-capping women, boycotting a woman in travail from medical aid, mobbing the widow as she returns from viewing the body of her murdered husband, driving from their calling all who will not obey the command of the village tyrant, mutilating dumb animals and cutting off the udders of cows, blowing up with dynamite public edifices in which a crowd of innocent sightseers of all ages and both sexes are gathered—these are not things which civilization reckons as liberties. They are not things by which any practical reform can be effected, by which any good cause can be advanced. America has seen something of Celtic lawlessness as well as Great Britain, and more Irish probably were put to death at the time of the draft riots in this city than have suffered under all those special acts for the prevention of crime in Ireland, miscalled coercion acts, the very number and frequent renewal of which only show that the British government is always trying to return to the ordinary course of law. Americans do not allow conspiracy to usurp the place of legal authority, or one man to deprive another of his livelihood by boycotting at his will; nor do I suppose that holders of real estate in New York regard with philanthropic complacency the proposal to repudiate rents. When the other European governments find it necessary to put forth their force in order to oppose disturbance, when Austria proclaims a state of siege, or Germany resorts to strong measures in Posen and Alsace-Lorraine, no cry of indignation is heard; when Italy sends her troops to restore order and crush an agrarian league which is dominating by assassination and outrage like that of Ireland, no American legislatures pass resolutions denouncing the Italian government and expressing sympathy with the Camorra. It seems to be believed that Ireland is governed as a dependency by a British Viceroy with despotic power, who oppresses the people at his pleasure or at the pleasure of tyrannical England. I doubt whether many Americans are distinctly conscious of the fact that Ireland like Scotland has her full representation in the United Parliament, and if her members would act like those ·from Scotland, might obtain any practical reform which she desired. The Lord-Lieutenant has been compared to an Austrian satrapy in Italy. An Austrian satrapy, with a full representation of the people in Parliament, a responsible executive, trial by jury, habeas corpus, and a free press! It happens that thirty years ago the British House of Commons voted by an overwhelming majority the abolition of the Lord-Lieutenancy of Ireland, but the bill was dropped, as Lord St. Germain, the Lord-Lieutenant of that day formally announced, in deference to the expressed wishes of the Irish people.

I do not blame Americans for misjudging us; the authority by which they are misled is apparently the highest. But they too know what faction is, and that in its evil paroxysms it is capable not only of betraying but of traducing the country. Americans will presently see that the dynamite of Herr Most and that of Rossa is the same; that the seeds of disorder and contempt for law scattered in Ireland will spring up here; that war between property and plundering anarchy impends in this as well as in other countries, and that you cannot strengthen the hands of anarchy in one country without strengthening them in all. Openly, and under its own banner, anarchism is making formidable attempts to grasp the government of American cities. It is not only your neighbor's house that is on fire and the flames of which you are fanning, it is your own. Nor ought Americans to forget that they have recently themselves set us an illustrious example. By them Englishmen have been taught resolutely to maintain the integrity of the nation, even though it be at the cost of the most tremendous of civil wars.

But then there is the social friction. At the time of the Revolution one ultra-classical patriot proposed that the language of the new Republic should be Latin, forgetting that Latin was the language of Nero and his slaves as well as of the Gracchi. I sometimes almost wish that his suggestion had been adopted, so that the two branches of our race might not have had a common tongue to convey their carpings, scoffings, and gibings to each other. English travellers come scurrying over the United States with notions gathered from Martin Chuzzlewit, seeing only the cities, where all that is least American and least worthy is apt to be gathered, not the farms and villages, in which largely reside the pith, force, and virtue of the nation; ignorant of the modes of living and travelling, running their heads against social custom, carrying about their own bath-tubs, and dressing as though they were among hunter tribes. Then they go home and write magazine articles about American society and life. Americans go to England full of Republican prejudice and sensitiveness, with minds made up to seeing nothing but tyranny or servility on all sides,— ignorant, they also, of the ways of the society in which they find themselves, construing every oversight and every word that they do not understand as a studied insult not only to themselves but to their Republic. I was reading the other day a book on British Aristocracy by a distinguished American, the lion's provider to one still more distinguished. He was so far free from prejudice as to admit that English judges did not often take bribes. But, in English society, he found a repulsive mass of aristocratic insolence on one side and of abject flunkyism on the other. The position of the men of intellect, the Tennysons, Brownings, Thackerays, Macaulays, Darwins, Huxleys, and Tyndalls he found to be that of the Russian serf, who holds the heads of his master's horses while his master flogs him. He represents the leaders of English society as going upon their knees for admission to his parties, which ought to have mollified him, but did not. It seems that when he was in England there was only one high-minded gentleman there, and even that one was in the habit of traducing the hospitality which he enjoyed. If people despise aristocracy as much as they say they do, would they be likely to talk quite so much about it? So far from the British people being the most abject slaves of aristocracy, they are the one nation in Europe which would never tolerate the existence of a noblesse and always insisted on the equality of high-born and low-born before the law. Aristocracy has survived in England for the very reason that there alone its privileges were closely curtailed and its arrogance was jealously repressed. In England, as in other countries, aristocracy as a political power is about to pass away, and there will be other and more rational guarantees of order and stability for the future. But I do not believe that the British aristocracy is worse than other rich and idle classes; I do not believe it is worse than the idle sons of millionaires in New York. It has at least some semblance of duties to perform. All its sins are committed under an electric light and telegraphed to a prurient world, which by its very craving for aristocratic scandal shows that it has a flunky's heart. As to the pomps and vanities of life they seem to me to be pretty much the same on both sides of the Atlantic. Assured rank, indeed, is less given to display than new born wealth. Surely all our studies of the philosophy of history and social evolution have not been utterly in vain. We ought to know by this time that in a land old in story and full of the traditions and relics of the past, beneath the shadow of ancient cathedrals, gray church towers, legendary mansions and immemorial oaks,— a land, of which the trim and finished loveliness bespeaks fourteen centuries of culture,—the structure of society cannot be the same that it is in this New World. We ought to have philosophy enough to admit that a structure of society different from ours may have graces, perhaps even virtues, of its own. The old cannot at a bound become as the new, nor would it be better for us if it could. Americanize the planet, and you will retard not quicken the march of civilization, which, to propel it, requires diversity and emulation. England may be politically behind America, and have lessons to learn from America which she will learn the more readily the more kindly they are imparted. But she is not a land of tyrants and slaves. Her monarchy does not cost the people more than Presidential elections. Good Mr. Carnegie, who deems it the special boon of Democracy that he is perfectly the equal of every other man, is no more politically the equal of a Boss than I am of a Duke. One liberty England possesses, unless my patriotism misleads me, in a degree peculiar to herself, and perhaps it is of all liberties the most vital and the most precious. During this Irish controversy, terribly momentous and exasperating as it is to us, Irish Nationalists and American sympathizers with Irish nationalism, have been allowed freely to express their opinions even in language far from courteous to Englishmen through all the magazines and organs of the English press. The English press is under the censorship neither of kings, nor of the mob. Perhaps the censorship of the mob is not less inimical to the free expression of truth, less narrowing or less degrading than that of kings.

The literary men of America, whose influence on sentiment must be great, are apt to be somewhat anglophobic. They have reason to feel galled by the unfair competition to which the absence of international copyright subjects them. I was reading, not long ago, an American book of travel in Italy, very pleasant, except that on every other page there was an angry thrust at England, where the writer told us he would be very sorry to live, though it did not appear that the presumptuous Britons were pressing that hateful domicile upon him. Then, after harping on English grossness, brutality, and barbarism, he goes to worship at the shrines of Byron, Keats, and Shelley; as though the poetry of Byron, Keats, and Shelley were anything but the flower of that plant, the root and stem of which are so coarse and vile. A Confederate flag is descried, floating probably over the home of some exile, on the Lake of Como. The writer is transported with patriotic wrath at the sight. Two Englishmen on board the steamer, as he tells us, grin; and he takes it for granted that their grinning is an expression of their British malignity; yet, surely, it may have been only a smile at his emotion, at which the reader, though innocent of British malignity, cannot possibly help smiling. "Heaven knows," a character is made to say in an American novel now in vogue, "I do not love the English. I was a youngster in our great war, but the iron entered into my soul when I understood their course towards us and when a gallant young sailor from our town, serving on the *Kearsage* in her fight with the *Alabama* (that British vessel under Confederate colors) was wounded by a shot cast in a British arsenal, and fired from a British cannon by a British seaman from the Royal Naval Reserve transferred from the training-ship *Excellent*." The writer shows that by the very way in which he strives to color the facts that he knows the charge here levelled against the British government and nation to be unjust; and art ill fulfills her mission when she propagates false history for the purpose of keeping up ill-will between nations.

The soldiers, by whom it might be supposed that the traditions of hostility would be specially preserved and cherished, I have usually found not bitter; but soldiers seldom are.

When Mr. Ingalls, or Mr. Fry, pours out his vocabulary upon England and upon us who rejoice in the name of Englishmen, I want to ask them, whether Ingalls and Fry are not English names. These gentlemen must have very bad blood in their own veins. Their education too must have been poor, if it is on English literature that their minds have been fed. The character of races, though perhaps not indelible, is lasting. It passes almost unchanged through zone after zone of history. The Frenchman is still the Gaul; the Spaniard is still the Iberian. Abraham still lives in the Arab tent. Yet we are asked by American anglophobists to believe that of two branches of the same race, which have been parted only for a single century, and have all that time been under the influence of the same literature and similar institutions, one is a mass of brutality and infamy, while the other is unapproachable perfection.

There has no doubt been a certain division, both of character and of achievement, between the Anglo-Saxon of the old country and the Anglo-Saxon of the New World. The Anglo-Saxon of the New World has organized Democracy, with the problems of which, after the Revolution, he was distinctly brought face to face; whereas the Anglo-Saxon of the old country, having glided into Democracy unawares, while he fancied himself still under a monarchy because he retained monarchical forms, is now turning to his brother of the New World for lessons in Democratic organization. With the Anglo-Saxon of the old country has necessarily hitherto remained the leadership of literature and science, which the race has known how to combine in full measure with political greatness. With the Anglo-Saxon of the old country have also remained the spirit of Elizabethan adventure and the faculty of conquering and of organizing conquest. Surely, in the British Empire in India, no Anglo-Saxon can fail to see at all events a splendid proof of the valor, the energy, the fortitude, and the governing-power of his race. Remember how small is the number of the Anglo-Saxons who rule those two hundred and fifty millions. Remember that since the establishment of British rule there has never been anything worthy the name of a political revolt, that at the time of the great mutiny all the native princes remained faithful, that when Russia threatened war the other day one of them came zealously forward with offers of contributing to the defence of the Empire. Remember that the Sikhs, with whom yesterday England was fighting desperately for ascendancy, are now her best soldiers, while their land is her most flourishing and loyal province. Yet we are told that the Anglo-Saxon can never get on with other races! It is not on force alone that the British Empire in India is founded; the force is totally inadequate to produce the moral and political effects. The certainty that strict faith will always be kept by the government is the talisman which makes Sepoy and Rajah alike loyal and true. In an American magazine, the other day, appeared a rabid invective against British rule by one of those cultivated Hindoos, Baboos as they are called, who owe their very existence to the peace of the Empire, and if its protection were withdrawn would be crushed like egg-shells amidst the wild collision of hostile races and creeds which would ensue. The best answer to the Baboo's accusations is the freedom of invective which he enjoys, and which is equally enjoyed by the native press of India. What other conqueror could ever afford to allow perfect liberty of complaint, and not only of complaint but of denunciation to the conquered? We, gentlemen of the Canadian Club of New York, heirs not of the feuds of our race, but of its glorious history, its high traditions, its famous names, can look with equal pride on all that it has done, whether in the Old World or in the New, from New York to Delhi, from Winnipeg or Toronto to Sidney or Melbourne, and rejoice in the thought that though the roll of England's drum may no longer go with morning around the world, and though the sun may set on England's military empire, morning in its course round the world will forever be greeted in the Anglo-Saxon tongue and the sun will never set on Anglo-Saxon greatness.

And if in the breast of any American envy is awakened by the imperial grandeur of his kinsmen in the Old World, perhaps there is a thought which may allay his pain. Power in England is passing out of the hands of the imperial classes, and those which gave birth to the heroic adventurers, into those of classes which, whatever may be their other qualities, are neither imperial nor heroic. It seems to be the grand aim of statesmen, by protective tariffs and ecoñomical legislation of all kinds, to call into existence factory-life on as large a scale as possible, as though this were one thing needed to make communities prosperous and happy. Wealth, no doubt, the factory-hand produces, and possibly he may prove hereafter to be good material for the community and the Parliament of Man, but he is about the worst of all material for the nation. He is apt to be a citizen of the labor market and to have those socialistic or half-socialistic tendencies with which patriotism cannot dwell. England has been inordinately enriched by the vast development of her manufactures. But for her force, perhaps even for her happiness, it would be better if Yorkshire streams still ran unpolluted to the sea and beside them dwelt English hearts. It seems at all events scarcely possible that such an electorate should continue to hold and administer the Indian Empire.

Some day we may be sure the schism in the Anglo-Saxon race will come to a end. Intercourse and intermarriage, which are every day increasing; the kindly words and acts of the wiser and better men on both sides; the influence of a common literature and the exchange of international courtesies and good offices—these, with all-healing time, will at last do their work. The growing sense of a common danger will cause Americans, if they hold property and love order, to give up gratifying their hatred of England by fomenting disorder in Ireland. The feud will cease to be cherished, the fetish of hatred will cease to be worshipped, even by the meanest members of either branch of the race. No peddler of international rancor will then be any longer able to circulate his villain sheets and rake up his shekels by trading on the lingering enmity of the Anglo-Saxon of the New World to his brother beyond the sea. But between the two branches of the race which the Atlantic divides, the only bond that can be renewed is that of the heart; though I have sometimes indulged a thought that there might at some future day be an Anglo-Saxon franchise, enabling a member of any English-speaking community to take up his citizenship in any other English-speaking community without naturalization, and that, in this manner, the only manner possible, might be fulfilled the desire of those who dream of Imperial Federation. But the relations of the English-speaking communities of Canada to the English-speaking communities of the rest of this continent are manifestly destined by nature to be more intimate. I do not speak of political relations, nor do I wish to raise the veil of the future on that subject; but the social and commercial relations of Canada with the United States must be those of two kindred communities dwelling not only side by side, but on territories interlaced and vitally connected in regard to all that concerns commerce and industry with each other, while united these territories form a continent by themselves. In spite of political separation, social and commercial fusion is in fact rapidly going on. There are now large colonies of Canadians south of the line, and Anglo-Saxons from Canada occupy, so far as I can learn, not the lowest grade, either in point of energy or of probity, in the hierarchy of American industry and trade. One name at all events they have in the front rank of American finance. Of those American fishermen, between whom and the fishermen of Canada this dispute has arisen, not a few, it seems, are Canadians. Not a little of Canadian commerce on the other hand is in American hands. The railway system of the two countries is one; and they are far advanced towards a union of currency. Of the old estrangement, which the Trent affair for a moment revived, almost the last traces have now disappeared and social reconciliation is complete. It is time then that the Anglo-Saxons on this continent should set aside the consequences of the schism and revert to the footing of common inheritance, instituting free-trade among themselves, allowing the life-blood of commerce to circulate freely through the whole body of their continent, enjoying in common all the advantages which the continent affords, its fisheries, its water-ways, its coasting-trade, and merging forever all possibility of dispute about them in a complete and permanent participation. The Fisheries dispute will have been a harbinger of amity in disguise if it leads us at last to make a strenuous effort to bring about a change so fraught with increase of wealth and other benefits to both countries as Commercial Union. The hour is in every way propitious if only American politicians will abstain from insulting or irritating England, whose consent is necessary, by reckless efforts to capture the Irish vote. Let us not allow the hour to pass away in fruitless discussion, but try to translate our wishes into actions. Nor need any Canadian fear that the political separation to which perhaps he clings will be forfeited by accepting Commercial Union. A poor and weak nationality that would be which depended upon a customs line. Introduce free-trade at once throughout the world and the nationalities will remain as before. Abolish every custom-house on the Pyrenees, France and Spain will still be nations as distinct from each other as ever. If political union ever takes place between the United States and Canada, it will not be because the people of the United States are disposed to aggression upon Canadian independence, of which there is no thought in any American breast, nor because the impediments to commercial intercourse and of the free interchange of commercial services will have been removed, but because in blood and character, language, religion, institutions, laws and interests, the two portions of the Anglo-Saxon race on this continent are one people.

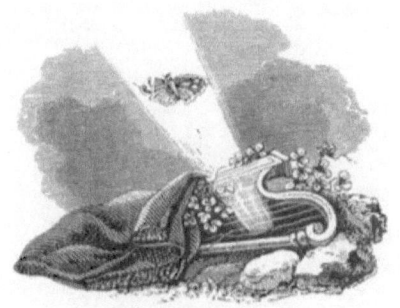

57'

"It is a land of rivers flowing free.
Lake-mirrored mountains, rising proud and stern,—
A land of spreading prairies ocean wide." J. H. Bowes

THE GREAT CANADIAN NORTH-WEST.

BY
REV. JOHN C. ECCLESTON, D. D.

{ Read before the Canadian Club
of New York.

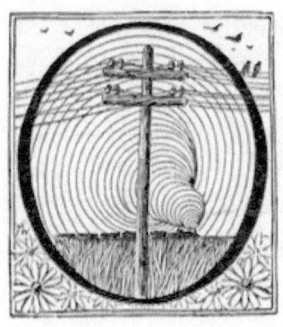

ONWARD has been the march of Canada in the path of progress through the development of its railway system and the enlargement of its canals. Therefore, and for two special reasons, I gladly accept the honor conferred upon me by your kind invitation to address you this evening upon "the resources of the Dominion of Canada—as developed by the recently completed Canadian Pacific Railroad."

First,—Because it affords me a fitting opportunity to acknowledge my personal indebtedness to Sir George Stephen, and Mr. W. C. Van Horne for their great kindness in extending to me the courtesies of their road, whereby I had the experience of a most thoroughly enjoyable summer vacation.

Second,--Because I am glad to have a chance to tell my countrymen of the "States" (for I am sure they are for the most part as ignorant as I was), some things they ought to know, something about this great Dominion of the North, just knit together by this Iron Nexus into one grand Confederation, reaching from ocean to ocean, and advancing with giant strides to imperial power.

We have been so long accustomed to see Canada figure on our maps as a narrow strip, with scattered villages and towns along the St. Lawrence and the great lakes, with innumerable smaller lakes and rivers, that it is difficult for us to realize that a rival nation, with a territory vastly larger than the whole American Union (not counting Alaska) and hardly eighteen years old, has arisen upon our borders, and like a young giant, set about making a glorious future for itself; building up great manufactories, levelling the mountains, filling up the valleys, bridging the rivers of the continent, digging canals, constructing thousands of miles of railroad, whereby to consolidate its empire, and make accessible its boundless natural resources of timber, mines and agricultural lands.

We are in the habit of laughing at the mistakes of English writers and tourists, concerning the geography of the United States, but this ignorance about America is not half so great as the ignorance of most of our people respecting a country which is at our very doors.

Art, Science, Literature, and Commerce. 61

The battle on the Heights of Abraham (Sept. 13, 1759) determined the ascendancy of the Anglo-Saxon race and tongue in America. When the news of Montcalm's defeat and death reached Paris, Voltaire, with his characteristic flippancy, said : " Well, we are well rid of 15,000 leagues of snow and ice."

Madame de Pompadour rejoiced, and said : " Now that Montcalm is dead, the King will have some peace"! But the people of France, who had gloried in the heroic deeds of Cartier, Champlain and De Salle, and the zealous labors of the martyred missionary fathers in the New World, mourned over the loss with a sore lamentation.

The Marquis de Choiseul, upon whom devolved the humiliating duty of signing the treaty of peace, was disconsolate. Turning to the British plenipotentiary, he said : " We shall be avenged : so long as France held Canada, your American colonies, needing your protection against a foreign power on their border, had to remain submissive, but now that you have driven us away, they will rebel against your authority, and assert their independence." We need not stop to relate how the Frenchman's prophecy was verified, how in process of time, the thirteen American colonies rebelled against King George, not that they loved the mother country (old England) *less*, but because they loved the liberties of Englishmen *more*, how during the terrible years of the revolution, the tide of a fratricidal war raged along the shores of the St. Lawrence and the great lakes.

But, all this is of the past. We rejoice that our lot has fallen on better days, that the strife of angry contention is forever ended—the sword supplanted by arbitration, and that henceforth, the only contest there can ever be between these two branches of the great Anglo-Saxon race, will be which of the two can best improve the magnificent inheritance God has divided between them in the western world.

MONTREAL.

The rattling of the train through the Victoria Bridge (one mile and three-quarters long), the master-piece of Brunell and Stephenson, announced our arrival at the city of The Royal Mount. By ten o'clock P. M., I was safely and most comfortably housed at the Windsor Hotel. I made the most of the three days I had for viewing the city, and could profitably have prolonged the time to a week, so numerous are its interesting sights and so beautiful its situation, that it is considered by many persons one of the finest cities on this continent.

Three miles of river frontage give ample room for shipping of every class. Back of it are, first long lines of warehouses and stores, then great massive public buildings and churches, and, further on, palatial mansions stretching westward to the foot of the mountain. Indications of a quiet, inobtrusive and substantial wealth are apparent on every side. It is asserted that there is no wealthier city area in the world than that which lies between the parallelogram made by Beaver Hall Hill and the foot of Mount Royal on the one hand, and Dorchester and Sherbrooke streets on the other. The view from the mountain, up and down the river, and over the Adirondack Mountains of the State of New York, and the Green Mountains of Vermont, is unsurpassingly grand and unique. The city claims 150,000 inhabitants. Here lived in former days the great feudal lords of the fur-trade: the McTavishes, the McGillimans, the McKenzies and the Frobishers, and other magnates of the Hudson Bay and the North-west companies, at the time of their greatest prosperity. It was at this spot that, from time to time, the Ottawas, Hurons, Algonquins and other tribes, who hunted the countries bordering on the great lakes, would come down the Ottawa river in canoes, laden with rich peltries, and barter them off for blankets, kettles, guns, knives, and all kinds of "fire-water," upon all which, the fur-lords were sure to make a profit of two or three hundred per cent. To-day, the Indian and the beaver, frightened alike by the scream of the iron horse, have retired to the inaccessible defiles of the Rocky Mountains, and the fur-lords have also vanished, but the beautiful city they had adorned and enriched still remains to challenge our admiration.

OTTAWA.

Before commencing our journey across the continent, journey which properly begins at Montreal, we will stop a few hours at the new and beautiful city of Ottawa, the political—as Montreal is the commercial—metropolis of the Dominion. Tossed backward and forward between Toronto, Kingston, Quebec and Montreal, the legislators of Canada have here found an abiding resting place. Ottawa is beautifully situated upon high bluffs, between the spray and roars of two headlong rivers, the Ottawa and the Gatineau. The Parliament buildings, which cover an area of four acres and which were erected at a cost of $5,000,000, are in gothic style of the XIIth century, unblemished by any surplus ornamentation. No edifices on this continent are more imposing and pleasing at the same time than these buildings. Built of a cream-colored sand-stone, the dressings are of Ohio free-stone, while the arches, over-windows and doors are of the warm Potsdam red-stone, a combination of colors most gratifying to the eye. Ottawa is the centre of the lumber interests. Last year the revenue of the Dominion from the rental and leases of its forest limits was $1,300,000. The number of feet of lumber cut was 1,600,000,000, representing a value of $58,000,000.

Among the far-seeing, anxiety is felt about the prodigious annual destruction of the forests, and they do not hesitate to declare that in twenty-five years at the present rate the lumber interest of the Dominion will be a thing of the past. One of the main causes of the forest waste, and one for the most part preventable, are forest fires kindled by hunters and others, who take no pains to extinguish their camp-fires or cover the embers with earth.

Pioneer settlers clear the land by setting the underbrush on fire; should a strong wind arise, the flames sweep onwards with a roar that is apalling. Great pine and cypress trees, of two and three hundred years of age, are shrivelled up like straws, the flames mounting almost in an instant from the roots to the topmost branches. The very surface of the soil is burnt up and the fiery hurricane, for thousands of acres, leaves nothing in its passage but hideous charred trunks, naked stones and mossless rocks. It is estimated that in 1881, the autumn fires in the Province of Ontario consumed $15,000,000 worth of timber.

THE ORIGIN AND INCEPTION OF THE CANADIAN PACIFIC RAILWAY.

The daily express leaves Montreal for Vancouver at 8 P. M., or 20 o'clock, as they call it; we take the sleeper at Ottawa, about midnight; but before doing so, there are several interesting preliminaries deserving our attention.

First, a word about the history of the railroad. As far back as 1851, a Company was projected at Toronto by Mr. Allen McDonald and the Hon. Henry Sherwood, by the name of the Lake Superior and Pacific Railroad. This, as well as similar schemes by the Hon. A. W. Morin and Mr. John Rose, came to naught, chiefly on account of the adverse report of Capt. Palliser who had been sent, in 1857, by the Imperial Government to survey and report upon the several proposed routes. After a four years' exploration, he pronounced the region of the Laurentides, around Lake Superior and the Lake of the Woods, impracticable for a railroad (speaking as an engineer), and the Rockies as an obstacle not to be overcome. He declared the central part of British America forever shut off by nature from both the Atlantic and Pacific seaboards. But Canada, having meanwhile consolidated her far distant and outlying provinces into a Federal Dominion, the question of binding these several Provinces together into some intimate and practicable union, became an urgent political as well as social and commercial necessity. Americanizing influences were in dangerous proximity at Winnipeg and Victoria. St. Paul and Portland and San Francisco were only a few hours distant; Ottawa was many weary days' journey remote.

It is unnecessary to dwell upon the interminable and fierce battles, the squabbles and scandals of the two rival parliamentary parties—the Liberal and Conservative; or among the greedy speculators who opened wide their mouths to swallow the big plum of 25,000,000 acres of the best wheat-land in the world, besides endless bonuses, and who gnashed and ground their teeth when they failed to receive them. When the Conservatives returned to power in 1878, the work of construction, meanwhile undertaken by the Government, was pushed forward with much energy, and the contract for the British Columbia section, the most difficult of all, was awarded to Onderdonk & Co. of New York.

In 1880, finding the labor too great, the Government wisely determined to put the construction of the road in the hands of a syndicate, which subsequently resolved itself into a Company. The syndicate was to receive from the Government 25,000,000 acres of land, $25,000,000 in cash, and sections 2 and 4 completed were given them as a present. The construction of all rival roads was prohibited for twenty years, all material for construction was to enter the Dominion free of duty, a free gift was made of all land required for workshops and stations, and an entire exemption of the whole property of the Company from taxation for twenty-five years. The road was, in consideration of these generous concessions, to be completed and put in running condition by May 1st, 1891.

The road is divided into four sections, and from Montreal to Callander it follows the old Canada Central Railroad.

Section First begins at Callander and ends at Port Arthur, 657 miles.

Section Second, from Port Arthur to Red River, 428 miles.
Section Third, from Red River to Sarona Ferry, 1,252 miles.
Section Fourth, from Sarona Ferry to Port Moody, 213 miles.
Total, 2,555 miles from Callander to the Pacific Ocean.

No sooner was the transfer to the syndicate accomplished than the work commenced with unparalleled vigor. The last rail was laid and the last spike driven on the 7th of November, 1885. Thus in the short period of five years or four years less than the contract with the Government called for, the road was thoroughly equipped and in running order.

CHARACTER OF THE ROAD AND ENGINEERING DIFFICULTIES.

More than 300 miles of the road have been cut through the hardest rock known to geologists—sienite and trap; mountains had to be tunnelled by the score; innumerable rivers of various sizes had to be spanned, some by iron bridges over a 1,000 feet in length; one by a wooden bridge 286 feet above the water—the highest structure of its kind in America. No less than fourteen streams had to be diverted from their natural beds, by tunnelling through the solid rock. The work went on summer and winter, sometimes the mercury stood at 30 and 40 degrees below zero. On the Lake Superior section there was at one time an army of 1,200 men, and 2,000 teams of horses, which were supplemented in winter time by 300 teams of dogs.

The entire line is thoroughly built with the best of

material, nothing was spared to make it first class in every particular.

The rails are of steel, and of English and Prussian manufacture.

The passenger equipment embraces many novelties not found elsewhere. The sleeping and dining-room cars are finished with rich upholstery, delicate carvings and antique brass-work, solid English comfort and artistic effect have been sought for in every detail. Bath-rooms, for ladies and for gentlemen, are provided in the sleepers, and luxurious accommodation for smokers. The fare in the dining-room cars is all that the most fastidious epicure could ask, choice fruits from California are furnished in season, all the way across the continent.

THE CANADIAN PACIFIC RAILROAD BRIDGE ACROSS THE ST. LAWRENCE.

I cannot omit drawing your attention to a great achievement in railroading that has been accomplished by the directors of the Canadian Pacific Railroad during the past summer, viz.: the bridge across the St. Lawrence, about one mile below the village of Lachine, where the river has a width of 3,300 feet and a depth of 40 feet. The construction of this bridge, which is only a few miles above the Victoria bridge, furnishes a fine illustration of the great progress made in the mechanical arts during the last twenty-five years. The " Victoria " costs $8,000,000 and six years were consumed in its construction, the " Canadian Pacific " has been completed in less than one year, at a cost of less than $1,000,000.

The masonry consists of two abutments and fifteen piers.

There are four land spans of 80 feet in length. Eight arches of 240 feet each, of the ordinary Pratt truss, span the river from both shores, while the channel portion of the river is crossed by two flanking spans of 270 feet in length, and two through "Cantilever" spans, each 408 feet long, these latter spans have an elevation of 60 feet above ordinary summer-water level.

The most difficult portion of the work was that of anchoring the piers of solid masonry on the rocky bed which, in some instances, was not only 40 feet below the surface but covered by a "hard pan" deposit 14 feet in thickness, which had all to be removed in a current of ten miles an hour. This difficult task was performed under the supervision of Mr. R. J. Reid of the firm of Messrs. Reid and Fleming. Original and most ingenious methods were resorted to. After the bottom had been carefully cleaned off with a dredge, a bottomless caisson made of square timber, with carefully caulked sides, was sunk upon the site of the pier; once sunk the small spaces between the rock and the bottom of the caisson were carefully packed by divers with bags of concrete. As soon as this was accomplished, large iron boxes containing two cubic yards of concrete were lowered inside the caisson, and by means of a crank acting upon a false bottom, the concrete was deposited in the caisson which on an average contained but one foot of water. The concrete was composed of one part Portland cement, one part sand and three parts broken stone. The day after the concrete had reached one-third the depth of the caisson, it was found sufficiently hardened to allow pumping and stop water from entering. After levelling this first course, it was then ready to receive the masonry, which in some cases lies at a depth of 25 feet from the water level. This system had the double advantage of avoiding the expense, risk and loss of time entailed by the use of coffer-dams of old; it gave a solid and durable bed for the masonry to rest upon,—a bed capable of resisting a head of 24 feet of water one day after its laying, and which, as time goes on, will certainly become as hard as rock itself.

To accurately anchor the caissons in such a rapid current was considered to be one of the most difficult operations of the whole work. This was effected with the aid of scows, anchors, chains and wire-ropes. For piers 13 and 14 these means were not considered sufficient and entirely practicable; therefore a rough crib in the shape of a truncated triangle was primarily sunk in front of those piers, the up-stream end of the crib was 10 feet long, the sides and lower end being 30 feet long, it was made of pieces of timber 10 inches apart, thus allowing the water to pass through and reducing the pressure of the current against it. These cribs were easily held in the rapid current, a small quantity of stone was afterwards brought to bear on their bottom, and as they were filled with stones, the latter stopped the current while offering at the same time greater resistance to the pressure of the water; when entirely filled these cribs formed a large eddy, behind which the permanent caissons were floated. The eddies were so strong that the caissons were forced up-stream, and instead of having to haul them against the current, it required a slight force to pull them down the stream into position.

Thus one of the most difficult problems in the construction of the bridge was solved in a cheap, rapid and satisfactory manner. When the tenders for the masonry were called for in October, 1885, requiring, under penalties, the completion of the foundations by the 30th of November, 1886, only three contractors bold enough were found to compete for the job. Engineers and others who had seen a similar work occupy the genius of a Stephenson and a Brunell six years for its construction, declared that it was utterly impossible to perform the work within the specified time. The steel for the superstructure was furnished by the Steel Company of Scotland, while the bridge proper was constructed by the Dominion Bridge Company of Lachine.

The whole of this great work has been executed under the supervision of chief engineer, P. Alex. Peterson; and Mr. E. Shaler Smith, member of the American Society of Civil Engineers, acted as Consulting Engineer for the superstructure.

[This portion of the lecture was beautifully illustrated by an outline drawing of the bridge kindly furnished by Mr. Van Horne, Vice-President of the Canadian Pacific.]

DIMENSIONS OF THE DOMINION.

I alluded in the beginning of my lecture to the ignorance of Americans respecting the geographical extent and resources of Canada.

Let us study for a few moments this fine chart of the Dominion, across which you see the track of the Canadian Pacific Railroad, as indicated by the black line passing over the two eastern provinces of Quebec and Ontario, covering 290,421 square miles, and stretching from the Gulf of St. Lawrence to the Red River; fasten your eyes upon the vast region once known as the North-western provinces purchased from the Hudson Bay Company in 1870, and now divided into four provinces: Assinaboia, 95,000 square miles; Saskatchewan, 114,000 square miles; Alberta, 100,000 square miles and Athabasca, 122,000 square miles. We have in these four provinces an area of 2,665,252 square miles, a region larger than all Russia in Europe, while the total area of the United States is but 3,547,000 square miles. The world is beginning to find out that this vast region which was once supposed to be forever abandoned to the beaver and the polar bear, really contains some of the finest wheat and grazing lands of the continent. I do not allude now to the comparatively well-known resources of Manitoba and Assinaboia, but of regions lying four hundred miles north of the Canadian Pacific Railroad, as far up as the Wild Peace River, where has been grown the No. 1 wheat which received the first prize at the Centennial Exposition in Philadelphia.

Again, look at this magnificent province of Manitoba, with its 123,200 square miles of area. Here are 75,000,000 acres, claimed by the enthusiastic "Winnipeggers" to be the wheat-field of the world, six million bushels of wheat found their way to the markets of the province last year. An expert estimates the average yield per acre throughout Manitoba at 18 bushels per acre, of which 95 per cent. will grade No. 1 hard. For 300 miles west of Winnipeg and for many miles on either side of the railroad, 95 per cent. of the prairie is excellent wheat-land, a rich black loomy soil of exhaustless fertility. In the Qu'Appelle Valley there is in successful operation a joint-stock farm of 64,000 acres (100 square miles). This year the proprietors expected to send 500,000 bushels of surplus wheat to the market. The Manitoba wheat is well known as being extremely hard, yielding 50 per cent. more than Minnesota wheat. There are physical causes for this. The further you travel towards the northern limit of its growth, the finer the quality of the soil you meet. The subsoil, throughout the intense heats and droughts of summer, is kept moist by the slow melting of the deep winter frosts; the moisture reaches up and nourishes the roots of the grain, and secures the crop, although the clouds may withold the later rains. Again, the sunshine in this land of the North is longer just at the needed time, when the ears are ripening. Heat alone will not bring wheat to maturity, solar light is also needed, and the greater its amount the better the result; and from the 15th of June to the 1st of July there are nearly two hours more day-light in Manitoba than in Ohio.

The valley of the Red and Assinaboine rivers alone are capable of feeding a population of many millions. Lord Selkirk was ridiculed, in 1812 when he said these "hyperborean alluvials would, some day, maintain a population of 30,000,000 souls." The child is born who will see Lord Selkirk's prediction realized. Immigrants are coming every day and from every part of the world, from Iceland and Russia, Sweden and Scotland; on foot and by steam, on horse-back and mule-back, and in the slow lumbering "ships of the prairie"—

> We hear the tread of pioneers of nations yet to be,
> The first low wash of waves where soon shall roll a human sea.

If Manitoba is to supply the world with bread, the succulent beefsteaks and blooded horses will come from Alberta. It is the ranch-ground of Canada, one vast area stretching from the Red Deer River and across the Bow Valley to the south of Belly River. We have reached here the foot of the great snow-capped Rockies, the backbone of the continent; but, to our surprise, there is in the air a warmth and a moisture different from anything yet experienced. The climate is more that of England than Canada; it is cooler in summer and warmer in winter than in the plains below and behind us. The "chinook" winds, wafting the moisture from the Kuro Siwo—or Japan gulf-stream of the Pacific Ocean—blow with regularity through the defiles of the mountains; their action so temperates the atmosphere during the winter that snow seldom accumulates to any great depth, or that severe cold weather prevails to any great extent, not to a sufficient extent to prevent cattle and horses from roaming, all the year round and uncared for, upon the thousand hills and surrounding valleys.

Calgary, the capital of Alberta, is admirably situated on a high plateau, at the junction of the Elbow and Bow rivers, from whence there is a superb view of the distant peaks and slopes of the mountains. It is about 65 miles from the Rockies, and 840 miles from Winnipeg.

The atmosphere is a marvel of purity and clearness, objects ten miles away appear to be only two miles distant. Words spoken in ordinary tones, at half a mile distance, can be heard distinctly. If I thought of emigrating to the Dominion, Alberta would certainly be my choice.

Finally, let us look at that great Province or empire, as

British Columbia might be justly called. Its area of 341,305 square miles, is larger than Great Britain and France combined, and five times as large as all the New England States. You see the road upon which we are to travel cutting across the three great mountain ranges that divide it: the Rocky, the Selkirk and the Gold. How audacious the attempt to run a train of cars over this seemingly inextricable tangle formed by raging torrents, treacherous glaciers and abrupt mountains, presenting the aspect as if a vast molten sea, lashed by titanic forces into gigantic billows, had been suddenly petrified at the extreme height of the storm!

Fifty years ago, this great Province was virtually unknown to the trappers of the Hudson Bay Company. In 1843 a fur-governor was stationed at Fort Camosun, now the beautiful city of Victoria, to receive the valuable pelts which the Indians brought in from the interior. Though it cannot yet be said of this Province that it is a land flowing with milk and honey, yet it is a beautiful country, endowed by nature with fertile fields, rich mines, the grandest scenery in North America, and a mild and salubrious climate.

EN ROUTE FOR VANCOUVER.

But let us retrace our imaginary steps, and begin at the starting point of our journey of five days and twelve hours.

Having secured at Montreal our sleeping accommodation through to the Pacific, we take the daily express train at Ottawa about midnight, and going immediately to bed, wake up the next morning to find the train skirting the shores of the beautiful Lake Nipissing. The Jesuit missionaries found the Indians residing around this Lake so beset with spirits and infested by demons, that they called it "The Lake of the Sorcerers." It abounds with fish of great size, affording fine sport for experts of the rod and reel; deer and cariboo are plentiful about its shores. Nipissing was repeatedly crossed by Champlain in his foreys against the Iroquois, and was in the direct line of communication used by the Hudson Bay voyageurs and its agents in their annual t ips from Montreal to Fort William.

During all of the next thirty hours we traverse a region forbidding to the eye; it is a puzzle to geologists and is destined for all times to be a cause of despair to the agriculturist. We are in the region of the "Laurentides" or "Laurentian Hills," that gigantic granite chain which rises on the coast of Labrador, and, after forming the northerly wall of the St. Lawrence Valley, sends one of its spurs down into the state of New York, where it towers up into the majestic Adirondacks, another spur circles the north shore of Lake Superior, whilst a third one sweeps northward and westward and finally sinks into the icy sea.

Professor Agassiz expressed the opinion that this Laurentian range was the oldest land on our globe, the first to lift its head above the primeval waters, and obey the almighty *fiat:* "Let the dry land appear." Vegetation has a hard struggle here with the rocks and crags, hewn into every shape by the storms of years, and the boulder-strewn beds of antidiluvian lakes and rivers; but stores of minerals of incalculable wealth lie buried in the bosom of these hills.

At Sudburg Junction (444 miles from Montreal) the much

abused "Algoma Mills" branch juts off, 93 miles to Georgian Bay. This branch road will be soon extended to Sault Ste.-Marie, and there will connect with the projected road from Duluth. The Canadian Pacific Company have opened at a point six miles north-west of Sudburg, copper mines of wonderful promise. The ores are sulphides containing an average of 16½ per cent. in copper. An expert says, "I feel safe in saying there are here two hundred million tons of ore in sight, and above the surface of the country."

As Port Arthur is approached, the glorious scenery of Lake Superior and Thunder Bay make an impression which the traveller will never forget. Thunder Cape, like a mighty janitor of the harbor, rises abruptly 1,400 feet above the lake. Across the water, the dark mass of the McKay's mountains looms up majestically, while Pie Island sits astride the mouth of the harbor like a huge Monitor at anchor. These three gigantic upheavals stand in massive dignity, like three emperors, each with a cloudy crown about his head.

Six miles from Port Arthur is the rival and once famous settlement of Fort William. When the North-west Fur Company was in its glory, Fort William was the place where the leading partners from Montreal proceeded in great state, once a year, to meet their agents and factors from the various trading-posts of the northern wilderness, to discuss the affairs of the Company and arrange plans for the future. Wrapped in rich furs, their huge canoes freighted with every convenience and luxury, and manned by Canadian voyageurs, these fur-lords ascended the Ottawa and the Matawan to Lake Nipissing, thence up the French River to Lake Superior.

They had a retinue of cooks and bakers, casks of choice wines, delicacies of every kind, in fact everything necessary for the banquets which were indispensable adjuncts of these great meets. In an immense wooden building was the great council hall and which also served as a banqueting hall, decorated with Indian arms and acoutrements, and trophies of the fur-trade from the Rocky Mountains to the Arctic Ocean.

There was a vast deal of solemn deliberation, hard Scottish reasoning and drinking. The tables groaned under the weight of game of all kinds: venison f.om the woods, fish from the lakes, with hunters' delicacies, such as buffalo tongue and beaver tail, and various luxuries from London, all served up by experienced cooks.

While the chiefs thus revelled in the Hall and made the rafters resound with bursts of loyalty and old Scottish songs, chanted in voices cracked and sharpened by northern blasts and blizzards, their merriment was echoed and prolonged by a mongrel legion of Canadian half-breeds, Indian hunters and vagabond hangers-on, who feasted sumptuously on the crumbs that fell from the tables, and made the welkin ring with old French ditties, mingled with Indian yelps and yellings.

The feudal state of Fort William is a thing of the past. Its banquet hall is deserted, its council chamber in ruins and the fur-lords of the lakes and forests have vanished forever like the buffalo and the beaver. Three hundred miles from Port Arthur, we reach Rat Portage, the capital of the enormous but not prepossessing district of Keewatin, the "country of the north wind," and the "Lake of the Woods'" station. This lake,—once supposed to be the source of the Mississippi River, and the starting-point for a boundary line in every treaty between Great Britain and the United States,—is 180 miles long and a veritable paradise for hunters, fishermen and the lovers of nature, in her inner sanctuaries. It is a favorite place for summer excursionists from Winnipeg, and unequalled as a place for camping parties.

Pierre Jaultier de Varennnes, Lord of Verendroge, built forts on the islands of this lake one hundred years before Lewis and Clark saw the waters of the "great river of the west." It was here one of Verendroge's sons, a Jesuit priest, and twenty men were massacred by the Sioux. The lake is so profusely dotted with islands that it seems, as it shifts and winds about in its devious channel, like a wondrously beautiful river.

Just half way across the continent, 1,434 miles from Montreal, 1,486 miles from Vancouver and 1,827 miles from New York, we reach the city of Winnipeg, the ambitious rival of Chicago. It is one of the "seven wonders" of the New World—whatever the other six may be; it is the central city of the continent and, probably within the very near future, one of the largest.

In 1870, when General (now Lord) Wolseley reached Manitoba to quell the Red River rebellion, all there was of Winnipeg consisted in a few huts and cottages erected by the pioneers close to the walls of Fort Garry, as a protection against the knives and tomahawks of the savages. To-day it is a proud city of 30,000 inhabitants, with substantial and beautiful buildings and churches, which would do credit to London and New York; it claims four hundred business houses; more than fifty manufacturing establishments, fifty good hotels and over a dozen banking-houses. Last year, 6,000,000 bushels of wheat passed through the Winnipeg elevators. Three daily papers furnish the citizens the news of the world. Six railroads center at Winnipeg and discharge at all hours of the day crowds of tourists, emigrants, farmers, merchants, and fill the streets with a busy, bustling concourse that reminds one of Broadway or Charing Cross. I spoke of six different railroads, but soon there will be a seventh, which, according to the sanguine projectors, is destined to revolutionize the traffic of the continent.

Sir Hugh Sutherland, President of the Manitoba and Hudson Bay Railway, promises that in two years' time trains will be running from Winnipeg to Churchill Harbor—Hudson Bay—a distance of 715 miles. From Winnipeg to Liverpool, via Hudson Bay, is but 3,641 miles, that is 783 miles less than by way of Montreal, and 1,052 miles shorter than by Chicago.

It is claimed by the projectors of this new route that it will considerably shorten the distance between the two great empires of the East and England's principal shipping port. Between Liverpool, China and Japan, a gain of 1,117 miles is made over the Montreal route, while a gain of 2,136 miles will be effected over the San Francisco and New York route. The new route will not only control the wheat traffic of all the north-western Provinces of the Dominion, but likewise that of Minnesota, Dakota, Montana and Washington Territory. The farmer shipping direct to Liverpool via Hudson Bay, will receive at least 15 per cent. more for his grain and save the interference of middlemen.

Time will prove the truth or fallacy of these fond hopes.

Deriding skeptics say that the first ship loaded with wheat that gets blocked up, and has to spend six months in the ice of Hudson Strait, will prick this bubble into flatulency. Others affirm that a safe and expeditious passage can be depended upon five months in the year.

Evidently Sir Hugh believes in the road, and as the government has guaranteed the interest on $5,000,000 worth of bonds, it is more than likely that the road will be completed.

The next step in order will be the building of a branch road to Fort Yukon; and that wonderful child, already spoken of, may yet see the iron horse careering down the valley of the Yukon and cooling his heels in the icy waters of Behring Sea.

Taking again our point of departure at Winnipeg, we have a stretch of 800 miles of prairie before reaching the foot of the Rockies. We pass on our way the thriving town of Brandon (which, before it was a year old, had grown into a city of 2,500 inhabitants), and reach Regina, the capital of the new territory of Assinaboia. Regina is the head-quarters of the "mounted police," the most efficient organized body of 500 men in the world—the terror of evil-doers in general and rumsellers and drinkers in particular.

Having already spoken in my preliminary remarks of the Province of Alberta, and its capital Calgary, we pause once more before climbing the mountains, at Bauff, which is destined, like the Hot Springs of Arkansas, to be the great sanitarium for rheumatic and other diseases of a chronic nature. Here, at a great elevation, surrounded by snow-clad mountains, we found hot sulphur springs of varying temperatures.

I met a man who told me that he had suffered such

tortures from chronic rheumatism that, despairing of relief, he had come to these springs resolved to kill himself if he did not find relief. After a few weeks bathing, his limbs relaxed from their fearful distorted condition, pain and agony subsided, and finally he was perfectly restored to health. The Canadian Pacific Railroad Company are erecting a first-class hotel on the spot, having every convenience for tourists and invalids, and unquestionably Bauff is destined for an important future.

OVER THE MOUNTAINS.

Forty-two miles from Calgary - up the Valley of the Bow River—we reach the foot of the hills, and the scenery becomes beautiful beyond description. At Padmore, 904 miles from Winnipeg, we are in the midst of the mountains, however the soil is still good and productive. The Stoney Indians, the best in the North-west, own large herds of cattle and horses, and hunt the wild-sheep and goats, the mountain-deer and the small fur animals of the mountain parks. Great mineral wealth is believed to exist in this portion of the route, not only gold and silver mines, but extensive and accessible coal-fields, both bituminous and anthracite.

The "Yellow Head" pass—far to the north of the present route and near the source of the Fraser river—was the point first chosen for crossing the Rockies, but after long and continued explorations the line was located thence down the North Thompson. However, after the road had been transferred to a syndicate by the government, an air-line from Winnipeg was decided upon, and the gap of the Bow River, known henceforth as the Kicking Horse River—so-called from the refractory steed of the engineer who mapped out the international boundaries—was the point finally chosen to cross the Rocky Mountains.

The adoption of this route saved 100 miles, while the road on that account was not more difficult to build nor more heavily graded than on the longer northern line, and its natural resources in land and minerals much greater. The highest peak above the pass was named Mount Stephen, after the President of the road. The bed of the road in the pass reaches an altitude of 5,300 feet above the sea-level, but its approaches from the east do not exceed the grade of 40 feet to the mile, save in the upper five miles of the Bow River where the rise reaches 75 feet per mile. The work of construction was easy through this pass.

The scenery here is grand beyond description, with beautiful peaks and abrupt mountains 5,000 and 6,000 feet high. It is generally cold at night, but the "chinook" winds do not allow the snow to remain long on the ground, save upon the summit of the mountains. Sometimes a heavy snow-storm is seen raging far above, while the sun shines in the valleys below.

The summit itself is a plateau four miles long dotted with three lakes. The first, going west, is Summit Lake, the source of Summit Creek; the second, Link Lake, seems to have neither exit nor entrance, no visible supply and no outlet; whilst the third and largest is the source of the noisy, impetuous Kicking-Horse River, which springs from its parent head, a wild, strong stream 50 feet wide, gaining in volume and speed as it rushes down the Kicking Horse Valley. Although the total length of this river is but 47 miles, its fall, until it finally merges with the broad Columbia, the great river of the west, is over 2,800 feet The railway follows the Kicking Horse River for 45 miles, and upon this plateau the work was not only extremely heavy, but the gradients and curves were more difficult than any yet encountered on the route. The lowest gradient obtained was 116 feet to the mile, or about 1 in 45; this rate of descent is maintained for 17 miles in one stretch. The heaviest work had to be performed upon the upper part of the plateau; here, in the distance of six miles, three tunnels of an aggregate length of 1,800 feet had to be constructed, and the Columbia had to be crossed three times. The work on the next ten miles was tolerably easy although the gradient was heavy; the lower part of the plateau has two or three tunnels of about 1,400 feet; the river is crossed no less than eight times, and the same heavy gradient, with curves of ten degrees, or 573 feet radius, had to be resorted to.

The road follows the Beaver River to the summit of the Selkirk range, which is 96 miles from the summit of the Rockies, and is about 1,000 feet lower, or 4,316 feet above sea-level. In the ascent the heavy gradient of 116 feet to the mile is again resorted to for about 16 miles, and then for 20 miles further on in descending the western slope.

At the head of the Loop, a magnificent glacier sweeps down almost to the very edge of the rails. More glaciers are seen in the distance, but this one towers upwards to the cloud line, just back of the station. A comfortable hotel is being erected at the foot of the glacier, where tourists can enjoy a refreshing sojourn and explore the mountain of ice.

The whole region between the main range of the Rocky Mountains and the Pacific is a vast disturbed rock formation.

For 800 miles in a north-west and south-east direction there is a valuable belt of metalliferous rocks, and in addition much of the country is heavily wooded. The Canadian Pacific Railway having penetrated here, the whole of this immense mining district has now a great future, and the gold of the Columbia and Kootenay rivers as well as the galena along Kootenay Lake is made accessible. The country lying around the mother lakes of the Columbia, and much of the Kootenay River valley, is interspersed with forest and prairie lands favorable to settlement, and admirably adapted for cattle raising. It only needs means of communication to make it equal to any part of the Dominion. The "bunch" grass, which grows constantly and is green at heart, even in mid-winter, is one of the most valuable pasture grass in the world, and is found everywhere in abundance, even at an altitude as high as 3,000 feet above the sea-level. The climate in the Kootenay district, from the Rocky Mountains to the Shuswap Lake, is very much like the mountainous portion of France, whilst west of the Rockies to the Pacific it compares favorably with that of the south of England.

The vast region surrounding the beautiful Shuswap Lake, close to the railroad Station of Sicamous, is a veritable haven for the lovers of the gun and rod; as much can be said of the district in the vicinity of the famous Okanagan Lake, which is reached by the same railroad station and thence by the Spilamacheen River. The water of these lakes is alive with fish, and their surface which is seen from the car-windows, is literally covered with swan, geese and ducks of every variety. The Okanagan region is also famous for its delicious bunch grass, and it is claimed that its valleys can produce the finest wheat in the world.

The tourist should not fail to stop at Yale, where the scenery is magnificently beautiful, affording all, in the form of raging torrent and snow-crowned mountain, that the most vivid imagination can paint. If time can be spared a visit to the once famous Cariboo gold mines, up the roaring Frazer River, will well repay the traveller. Here may be found wild mountain scenery unsurpassed for grandeur on our globe, and yet in the midst of this wildness there is a vegetation luxuriant in freshness. Wherever there is a crevice, even at the very base of the snow-clad peaks, are found clumps of the beautiful Douglass pine; lower down, and wherever a handfull of soil can rest, are myriads of wild-flowers and lilies of the valley.

Skirting further on the north bank of the Frazer River to within a few miles of New Westminster—where the river leaves the Frazer Valley and crosses the lowlands of the Pitt River marshes—the road reaches Port Moody, at the extremity of the southern arm of Buward Inlet. The grand terminus of the Canadian Pacific Railway is established at Vancouver, six miles further down the Inlet, where the government of British Columbia has given the railroad company a tract of land nine square miles in extent. Here is the prospective site—as I was told—of the great metropolis of the Pacific coast, a contemplated rival of San Francisco. I was offered a building lot 25x50 feet, with the primitive forest still standing on it, for $1,000, but I did not purchase it. Meanwhile, as an injunction at present hinders the train from running through to Vancouver, we have to take the steamer at Port Moody for Victoria, 75 miles distant across the Gulf of Georgia, which is, for all passengers, the real terminus of the road.

VANCOUVER ISLAND.

The *termini* question of the Canadian Pacific Railway has been a cause of great anxiety to dwellers on the Pacific slope of the Dominion, and the occasion of no little bad blood on the part of disappointed speculators. Sir John A. Macdonald, with his wonted astuteness, essayed to cut the gordian-knot at a reception given him by the people of Victoria last August.

" We are not, said he, to be limited to Halifax, Quebec, Montreal or British Columbia, whether it be Port Moody or Victoria—the termini of the Canadian Pacific Railway are Liverpool and Hong-Kong ! "

Victoria, the chief city of the island, and the capital of the Province, is a charming place ; it has a population of 12,000 which is increasing rapidly. Founded in 1843 by the Hudson Bay Company, it received the name of Fort Camosun. In 1845, in honor of the Prince Consort, the name was changed to that of Albert, but later on and in the same year, it was definitely named Victoria.

In 1857-58, the discovery of gold on the main-land attracted crowds of adventurers, and Victoria experienced the same kind of "boom" that cursed Winnipeg in 1882. Thirty thousand gold hunters from California and the American territories invaded the Province, and made incursions into the wilds of the Frazer River placers. The destruction of the fur-trade and the almost total disorganization of society were the results of this invasion. A few hundreds—surviving to famine and every hardship—secured bags of gold; but the rest perished miserably, or drifted back to Victoria, demoralized and ruined. During this period of aggressive rowdyism, the main-land was constituted into a colony.

In 1866, Vancouver Island was legislatively united to the main-land and the name of British Columbia was given the colony, which became in 1871 a Province of the Dominion. Until the first train from Montreal arrived at Port Moody, the Union was little better than one on paper; but now, with daily trains bringing mails and passengers in twelve days from England, with her three hundred miles of gold-bearing quartz mountains, her splendid harbors, her coal-fields, her fisheries and forests, the future of British Columbia is assured. She is destined to gravitate to the very front rank of the communities on the Pacific, if not to become some day the stiongest and richest Province of the Dominion.

The climate of Victoria is the most equable in the world. The winter is especially mild, the mercury seldom reaching the freezing point. The summer is temperate, heat seldom rising above 72°. Southerly winds prevail two-thirds of the year. Summer lasts from April to October; flowers bloom out-doors the whole year. And yet in Victoria we are here six degrees north of Quebec, in latitude 50. The softness of the climate is due to "Kuro Siwo," which brings the warmer temperature of the Japan and China seas, in the same way as the gulf-stream tempers the climate of the British Islands. The weather of

Vancouver Island is said by those who have thoroughly tested the matter to be milder and more agreeable than that of the south of England, the summers longer and finer, the winters shorter and less rigorous.

The harbor proper of Victoria is small, with a difficult pass; but the adjacent harbor of Esquimault, across a narrow neck of land, affords all the requisites of a first-class naval station. The Imperial Government is spending large sums here, and in the outer royal-roads the largest men-of-war can ride safely.

At an early future Esquimault will undoubtedly be the emporium of an immense trade with the Asiatic ports, and fortnightly lines of first-class steamers, subsidized by the Home Government, will ply regularly between Victoria, Hong-Kong and Australia.

The coast fisheries are almost illimitable, and their capabilities have hardly been put to contribution; yet, the principal species are halibut, salmon, cod and herring. In some of the narrow estuaries and bays, at flood-tide the water is so densely packed with salmon struggling to reach a spawning-ground, that it is actually possible sometimes to lay boards upon the backs of the swarms and walk over dry shod. Halibut, from 100 to 500 lbs., are common. For ten cents Indians will furnish enough fish to feed ten men. Herring are raked out of the water by boat loads.

Here is a grand and exhaustless industry awaiting development; and, as if Providence had designed to indicate a way to utilization, salt-springs of great value, yielding 3,446 gr. of salt to each gallon of water, have been discovered near Nanaimo.

It would pay the Dominion Government a handsome dividend to transport bodily the starving population of the icy coasts of Labrador to the prolific shores of British Columbia.

Some day the wheat-fields of Manitoba may become exhausted and refuse to yield their tribute; the forests of Ontario and Quebec may perish before the woodman's axe and the devastating flames, but the riches of the ocean are inexhaustible, and each recurrent tide will bring to the inhabitants of this favored land abundant food.

Ladies and gentlemen, I have detained you longer than was my purpose, but my excuse for this encroachment upon your patience and comfort lies in the fact that even a partial development of the subject under consideration was out of proportion to the one-hour time to which I should have confined myself. I may have been incoherent and sometimes perhaps inconsequential in my remarks; but I shall be content if I have succeeded, even in an imperfect degree, in diffusing a knowledge of what Lord Beaconsfield once happily phrased: "The boundless regions and illimitable possibilities of the great North-west."

In concluding, I may be permitted to remark to the members of the Canadian Club of New York, that my countrymen, the great people of the United States, entertain no petty jealousies for such noble competitors as I have told you of to-night, but taking only into account the good secured, they hail with joy the opening of this new route to the riches of the mighty West. The honors of knighthood were never more worthily bestowed by royalty upon any subject, than by Her Majesty Queen Victoria upon the President of the Canadian

Pacific Railroad, Sir George Stephen, in recognition of his great abilities and persevering industry in bringing this great work to so speedy and happy a completion.

91

THE HUMOROUS SIDE OF CANADIAN HISTORY.

BY

J. W. BENGOUGH, *Editor Toronto Grip.*

Read before the Canadian Club of New York.

CAN I convey to you, in the hour at my disposal, as much solid information as you may be in need of? Probably yea, because the lectures given in this course, under the auspices of the Canadian Club, have naturally pertained to that glorious country, Canada. But, so far as I am aware, no speaker has yet dealt systematically with the history of Canada.

Pending the arrival of Mr. Goldwin Smith, who is at present engaged umpiring for the foot-ball club at Cornell, I propose to devote my hour to the subject suggested, and in case Mr. Smith should feel offended by my intrusion into his special domain, I will endeavor to mollify him in advance by making a pretty portrait of him right here. [A rapid sketch here set forth a picture at once recognized by the audience as —not Goldwin Smith—but Mr. Whitelaw Reid.]

Perhaps, before going on, I ought to apologize to the American portion of my audience for not having chosen a theme of greater novelty to them than the History of Canada. I had anticipated an audience made up chiefly of Canadians, but it is too late now to rectify the mistake. I am well aware that the citizens of the United States are just as familiar with Canada, her history and her affairs, as they are with Chinese Tartary, and I can hardly hope to tell them anything they do not know. But in view of the fact that Canada and the Republic have many features in common, besides baseball, and that many more or less distant relatives of American citizens are residing in that country, having in a few cases been struck somewhat suddenly by its charms as a place of residence, and having since exhibited a clinging affection for it, which few native Canadians can rival, it seems to me that all will be interested in the theme I have selected.

Canada is the name given to the greater portion of the continent of North America, and politically it is an integral portion of the British Empire. I mention this because there is an impression prevailing in Ohio and some other foreign countries, that Canada is owned by a railway syndicate. This is a mistake. Nominally Canada belongs to Great Britain, it contributes the adjective to the title, as Britain itself is only a small affair, but really and practically the vast Dominion is owned and run by the handsome and picturesque people so well represented in blanket suits on the present occasion. [Alluding to the uniformed snowshoers ranged upon the platform.]

' I may just remark here, *en passong*, as they say in Montreal, that the Canadian people when at home, invariably dress in the costume here shown, just as the people of New Jersey wear long-tailed coats and short breeches with straps to them, and bell-crowned beaver hats, with stars on their waistcoats and stripes on their pantaloons. It's the national costume you know, but they rarely venture out of the country with such good clothes on. When a Canadian makes up his mind to settle in New York, he invariably adopts the New York style of dress. He changes his clothes at the border, and then he goes in like a regular American, to Wall Street "born." Before long, so far as outward appearance goes, he would pass for a native New Yorker, and you could only tell he was a Canadian by contemplating the number of islands he owns and the magnitude of his ferry franchises. And this leads me to remark that when M. Bartholdi dressed that statue of his in Greek clothing, he availed himself of a poetic license. Canadians of the sterner sex *never* dress that way, never. To illustrate this point I will here make a rough sketch of the statue, as pictures of it are so rare in this city that its shape may have escaped your memory. Not only in the matter of costume, but also in the features, Bartholdi, with true French *naïveté*, endeavored to conceal the fact that in this great work of art he was paying a delicate compliment to a Canadian. He was afraid Mr. Wiman mightn't like it if made too literal. For I suppose it is pretty well known by this time that the statue is really meant for Wiman. The very fact that it stands there bossing an island is enough to suggest this, even if Bartholdi had never confessed his real design. To be sure, mustache and mutton-chops do not look well in bronze, but they're all right on paper, and they're necessary in this case to expose Bartholdi's pleasant allegory. All that remains to be changed now is the legend, which is not

" Liberty Enlightening the World," but " Wiman Defying New Jersey."

This, however, is a digression from our historical subject. Canada was discovered by Jacques-Cartier, while engaged in a fishing cruise around the banks of New Foundland. From the banks to Canada would seem to be an unerring impulse of the

Art, Science, Literature, and Commerce. 97

human mind. It is not true, however, that Cartier is French for *cashier*, and time has fully vindicated this gentleman's character, as the banks of New Foundland are to-day as sound as ever. The coincidence was startling, it must be confessed, and we can therefore excuse the newspapers of the day for hinting that there was something fishy about his sudden departure.

This event occurred some time after Christopher Columbus had got in his work. And Columbus, by the way, as an illustration of patience and perseverance is worthy even of the study of those good Democratic statesmen who are waiting for Cleveland to "turn the rascals out." I don't know what Columbus looked like, but I feel sure that upon his countenance was stamped a calm tranquil expression that no delays and discouragements could change. If so, he didn't look much like this. [Here a wild-looking sketch of Mr. C. A. Dana was given.]

Consider what Chris had to go through before he got started on that memorable voyage to India. It took him just twenty years to get started. Now, if it had been that he had to wait for Mrs. C... to get dressed, we wouldn't have wondered so much. But the trouble wasn't of that kind, it was purely financial. He couldn't sail without raising the wind, and mark his wonderful patience in raising it. Twenty years. The trouble was, nobody believed in his scheme as sound, and in the public interest. If it had been a surface-line franchise he was after, he might have convinced the Aldermen, but Christopher wasn't *Sharp*. It never occurred to him to get the ladies of the Congregation to go around with the book, though as a matter of fact he succeeded at last by the aid of a lady, Queen Isabella of Castile, whose name is to this day a sweet smelling savor, embalmed in an immortal kind of soap, "Matchless for the complexion.— Yours truly, LILY LANGTRY."

Columbus went from court to court after the boodle, it's a way boodlers have of going from court to court, if you notice—and at last he found a friend in Ferdinand. Ferdinand had a lot of the proceeds salted down, as was generally suspected, and he gave Columbus a check for the required amount, remarking, "Go West, young man, and grow up with the country." Thus was patience rewarded. The voyage was a severe one, everybody was sick of it and mutinied. Columbus stood on the quarter deck with his guitar and sang to the moon about everything being at sixes and at sevens. A bird alighted on the topmast! Omen of success: Land must be nigh. With one rapid glance the piercing eye of Columbus seizes the happy portent. The fact that it was an *Eagle* proved that land must be near; while the shield of stars and bars upon its breast, the Canada codfish falling from its talons, the ninety-cent dollar hanging from its neck, and finally its piercing cry of *E Pluribus Unum* proved that that land could be no other than America, where all men are born free and equal, but don't stay so. America was discovered; no longer could it bashfully avoid the gaze of the other nations, and it doesn't.

Columbus' work made a boom in the discovery business, and that's how Cartier happened to be around in time to discover Canada. Cartier was a Frenchman, and he handed over the country to the king of France, as a matter of course. This one action is enough to show that Cartier had no connection with the Standard Oil Company; but his simplicity in giving away the country when he might have kept it himself has modified Mr. Gould's opinion of his otherwise admirable character. This was the first time Canada was given away. The

offence was repeated, I've heard, at the time of the Washington treaty. Public opinion over there is opposed to this, as a regular thing, and at present there is a disposition to conserve the public interests, as it were. Perhaps I can convey the idea with a sketch.

When Mr. Cartier first landed in Canada there were Indians there. I do not wish to pose as a sensationalist, nor to rudely upset your settled convictions for the mere purpose of startling you, but I do allege that there were more Indians in Canada then than there are now. Several more. In fact, the majority of the present inhabitants are *white*, though President Cleveland seem to think our Government doesn't act that way.

The fact is the Indians are comparatively scarce now. They don't any longer pitch their tents in the main streets of Toronto, Montreal and Quebec. Most of them have been killed, though they still persist, the survivors, in playing Lacrosse. Had foot-ball, I mean the Yale and Andover variety, been known amongst them, the race would no doubt have been extinct. Then politics has no doubt helped to exterminate the Red Man. An Indian can eat most anything, but he must have pure air, and when the party caucus was established in Canada, the Indians had to go further back. You never find any Indians in the lobby at Ottawa. They couldn't stand it. I am informed that Indians take an active part in politics of Tammany Hall in this city, but that only shows that pure, mugwumpy politics isn't so fatal to them as the corrupt kind. At the same time I suspect that the Tammany politicians are not really Indians of a delicate type. In Cartier's time the population of Quebec was sixty, that is the pale-face population. As the uncivilized red men ruled on both sides of the St. Lawrence in those days, it is not likely that there were refugee defaulters. The Indian is pretty mean, but he isn't mean enough to have an extradition law that protects that sort of thief from justice.

These white men were honest French voyageurs, but

there are probably sixty of the other fellows in Quebec to day. Such is progress and civilization.

The manners of the early Indian tribes of Canada are very interesting. Their way of bringing up children, for example, was peculiar. The infant was strapped to a board and placed against a tree outside of the tent. This kept the youngster straight, which is more than the modern white method does : and besides it inured the child to the hardships of boarding out. I might also mention the Indian system of writing. In signing treaties, they used symbols for their names, thus the Great Chief Wise-Owl-Who-sees-in-the-Dark, would sign in this way. [Here a rough outline sketch of an owl was given].

Now such a signature wasn't much as a work of art, but it was worth more on a treaty generally than the white man's. In too many cases the words our Canadian poet *Mair* has put into the mouth of an Indian character were true :

> " Our sacred treaties are infringed and torn,
> Laughed out of sanctity, and spurned away,
> Used by the Long Knife's slave to light his fire
> Or turned to kites by thoughtless boys, whose wrists
> Anchor their fathers lies in front of Heaven !"

This Indian method of conveying ideas by means of pictures, is a great scheme, and is now in vogue in the highest journalistic circles. It forms the basis in fact, of the colossal and well-earned fortunes of Messrs. Keppler, Nast, Gillam, Opper, De Grimm, Hamilton, Zimmerman, Taylor and many other smart young men well known to you all. Of course in their hands it is greatly improved. They color their symbols more or less gaudily, and sell them for ten cents a copy. And they finish them up better than the Indian artist used to. For instance, in this case they would put on the modern improvements in this way, and call it, Wise-Man-Looking-Two ways-for-a-Presidential-Nomination. [An owl was here transformed into General B. F. Butler.]

The institution known as the lodge was universal among the aborigines, and one of their most striking characteristics was a fondness for display in the matter of dress. Nothing so tickled the untutored child of the forest as to be rigged in regalia, with feathers, sashes and ribbons, and the letters A. F. & A. M., or I. O. O. F., or other mysterious symbols be-spangling his bosom. In such a costume he thought nothing of fatigue, but would willingly travel on dusty roads all day in the hottest weather. When the savage denizens of Hochelaga (now Montreal) wanted to go on the war-path, they would just stick orange lilies in their hair and marched through that village on July 12th. That was all that was necessary.

The Indian women didn't have a vote, but the men folks let them carry everything by acclamation, especially tent poles and camp-fixtures, and they never endeavored to deceive them by subsequently chewing cloves. In vain Miss Anthony, who arrived a little before Cartier, advocated the female franchise and dress reform. No doubt the latter was needed, as you will see when I roughly sketch the costume then in vogue. To show that the absurdity was not confined to one sex, I will try to give you an idea also of the costume of the young bucks of the Iroquois tribe. [Here an amusing caricature of an Indian dude and dudene was given.]

Art, Science, Literature, and Commerce.

The domestic arrangements of the Canadian Indians were, as we might reasonably anticipate, no better than those of other barbarian people. They were especially faulty, however, on the very important subject of marriage.

In the first place the courtship was peculiar. Sometimes the principal parties were not consulted at all. The young woman's mamma simply took a fish pole and went abroad to catch whatever she could in the shape of a man. No mere Indian, however handsome, had any chance while there were young lords and counts visiting at Cartier's house. The Indian girls were just crazy after blue blood, but sometimes they eloped with a low down Indian, because then the papers always described them as beautiful and accomplished. There is no mention in this early history of divorce proceedings, and so we are left in the dark as to how ladies, without talent even, became actresses in those days.

The Indians had two very noticeable vices, gambling and cruelty. As to the first it is alleged that in the excitement of the game (Stock Exchange or whatever they called it), players often staked their lives on the result, whence no doubt is derived the phrase : " You bet your sweet life." Their cruelty was proverbial, they were the original inventors of the spoils system, and after a victory they tortured and scalped their captives without any fine distinction as to offensive partisanship. I am glad to say this is no longer the practice in Canada. We now enjoy civil-service reform and the victorious party doesn't murder its enemies. It only removes them from office.

To return to Jacques-Cartier, he appears to have been a

man of great magnetism and chivalry, as he earned the popular title of the *Plumed Knight* amongst the simple and unsophisticated aborigines. Just here it might be interesting to introduce his portrait, which I have copied from historical documents discovered in Maine. Maine at that time belonged to Canada you know, and does yet by rights, some folks say. [Here a portrait of Jas. G. Blaine.]

Cartier was succeeded by a long train of other French gentlemen whose deeds I have not time to dwell upon. At length, the country passed into the hands of the British, after some preliminary ceremonies on the plains of Abraham, near Quebec. You are familiar, of course, with the incidents of that memorable battle, and especially with the last words of Wolfe, which are so often quoted. Somebody said to him: "They run." "Who run?" he asked. "The Republicans." "Then I die happy," he replied.

I think that was it, if I haven't got it mixed with the third-party vote in Pennsylvania in November.

The British flag was still waving over the land when I left. Attempts have been made on a couple of occasions to put a showier piece of bunting in its place, but without success. A certain Republic, which shall be nameless, had something to do with the attempts I refer to. If you had only told me of your intention I could have saved you a great deal of worry and expense by informing you that the Canadians cannot be conquered by force of arms. I don't blame you for trying though, for everybody who knows what Canadian girls are like would be anxious to conquer or perish just as you were. It is a tribute to American shrewdness, however, that you have dropped the military plan, and resorted to this present scheme. I have no doubt your calculation is correct that as soon as the absent boodle aldermen and bank presidents form a majority of our population over there, they will cast a solid vote for annexation on condition of a general amnesty being granted. And I have only this to say, that as soon as a clear majority of our most wealthy citizens so decide, annexation will be all right. But I see that my time is up, and I must drop this interesting theme and bid you good night.

105'

"I love Quebec for three good reasons, one; Her matchless beauty that so takes the eye. Her famous history in the years gone by,— And last for sake of him, her worthy son, Bone of her bone, whose facile pen has run Through tomes of legendary lore." — W. KIRBY.

THE HEROINES OF NEW FRANCE.

BY
J. M. LEMOINE, F. R. S. C.

{ *An address delivered before the Canadian Club of New York.* }

CERTAINLY, your cordial greeting this evening overcomes much of the diffidence I felt in making my first bow to a cultured New York audience. However, in your presence, I feel as if I required but scant apology for my subject: The noble devotion to duty of three of the remarkable women, whose brave deeds have illumined the early times of Canada.

This evening, I witness what to a Canadian is a very gratifying spectacle: an array of Canada's most hopeful sons, striking out boldly and successfully as merchants, manufacturers, professional men, writers, in fact an arrray of energetic men invading every important path open to the human intellect and human industry in this great metropolis of the western world.

Had I to dilate on the patriotism of De Longueuil; the daring achievements of his worthy brothers d'Iberville and De Ste.-Hélène; the self-sacrificing Dollard des Ormeaux and his Spartan band of heroes; the saintly memories of Jogues, De Brébœuf and L'Alleman; the lion heartedness of grim old Count de Frontenac, answering admiral Phips from the mouths of his cannon, as well as of other worthies whose careers constitute, according to a well-remembered Vice-Roy of ours, Lord Elgin, what he happily styled "the heroic era of Canada," easy would be my task, ample the material.

The pregnant though silent past abounds with grand figures in our historical drama; of men illustrious in life, glorious in death! But it is not my purpose to entertain you this evening with man's prowess in the early history of Canada. My object is to recite to you the plain and unvarnished tale of three of the purest, bravest and most devoted women that have illustrated the early part of our history, whose heroic deeds cast a guiding-hallow in the path of toiling and tottering humanity, and to whose spotless record thinking men cannot remain indifferent.

We have had on our side of the frontier, as you have had on yours, several noteworthy women, who have left their footprints on the sands of time.

One of the first recalled is the helpmate of the dauntless

founder of Quebec, Hélène Boullé, the girlish-bride won by Samuel de Champlain from her gay and refined Parisian home, and whose sweetness later on, in 1620, made fragrant Canadian wilds.

On the 5th December, 1610, Champlain was wedded to Mademoiselle Hélène Boullé, whose father, Nicolas Boullé, was private secretary in the King's household. The damsel had not yet attained her twelfth year; she had been brought up a Calvinist, the faith of her father. Her mother, Marguerite Alixe, originally a Roman Catholic, had also espoused her husband's creed: but presently we shall see the youthful Hélène adopting Champlain's religious tenets and becoming, in later years, quite an enthusiast in her newly-pledged faith.

It was soon rumored that the daring founder of Quebec had not only won the hand of a handsome, high-born French girl, but also the heart of an heiress: 4,500 livres of her dowry of 6,000 livres were forthwith placed at the disposal of her liege lord to fit out vessels for his return to Quebec. However, it does not appear that until her landing in Quebec, the youthful bride had seen much of her elderly husband, who was constantly engaged about 1618 in distant sea-voyages, land explorations and Indian wars. Champlain spent two years in France, and having realized upon all he possessed there, he persuaded his spouse, who had then attained her twenty-second year, to accompany him to Canada. She cheerfully consented, taking with her three maids-in-waiting.

Intense was the joy of the struggling colonists at the return of their brave Governor, their trusted and powerful protector;

great was their admiration of the winsome and lovable wife that accompanied him.

The first lady of Canada very soon realized what meant a Quebec home in 1620. It was a life of incessant alarms, with scurvy and periodical famines for the colonists; of gluttony and pagan rites, of debauchery on the part of the greasy, naked and uncouth savages hutted round the fort.

Within two years after Madame de Champlain's arrival, a large band of Iroquois hovered on the outskirts of Quebec. The recollection of the fatal effects of Champlain's arquebuse alone deterred them from raiding the town. One day Champlain and the greater portion of his men being absent, the war-whoop was sounded; the women and children shut themselves in the fort, the Recollet Convent on the banks of the St. Charles was assailed. The friars fortified their quarters, and made a bold front; the Iroquois retired after capturing two Hurons, whom they tortured and burnt. Judge of the alarm of the gentle deserted lady in the fort and of her French maids. For four successive winters January storms and prowling Indians had gathered round the battlements of the grim old fort, and still Madame de Champlain remained firm at her post of duty.

One of her favorite occupations was that of ministering to the spiritual and temporal wants of the Indian children, and visiting them in their wigwams. Soon she appeared, in their simple and grateful eyes, as a species of superior being; they felt inclined to worship her. History recalls the charms of her person, her winning manners, her kindliness. The Governor's lady, in her rambles in the forest, wore an article of feminine toilet not unusual in those days: a small mirror hung to her side. The savages took particular delight in seeing their swarthy face reflected in the magical glass. It appealed irresistibly to their simple nature: "A beauteous being, they said, who watched over them in sickness, who loved them so much as to carry their image close to her heart, must be more than human." Blessings and offerings attended her footsteps.

The graceful figure of the first lady of Canada gliding noiselessly, more than two centuries ago, by the side of the murmuring waters of the wild St. Lawrence, a help-mate to her noble husband, a pattern of purity and refinement, was indeed a vision of female loveliness and womanly devotion for a poet to immortalize.

Daily alarms, solitude, isolation from the friendly faces of her youth, soon began to tell on the forlorn *châtelaine*. Four years of existence in this bleak wilderness was too much for the high-born dame, nurtured amidst the amenities of Parisian *salons*. She longed for the loved home beyond the seas. In her dreams another solitude had been revealed to her: the mystic solitude of the cloister, where, undisturbed, she might send up her prayers on high for her absent husband.

One bright August morning in 1624, [the 15th], all Quebec sorrowfully watched the sails of a white-pennoned bark, receding beyond Pointe Levi, conveying to less lonely climes the released captive....

Nineteen years after the death of her valiant knight, Madame de Champlain founded at Meaux, in France, a Convent of Ursulines nuns, to which she retired. On the 20th December, 1654, her gentle spirit took from thence its flight to less evanescent scenes.

We shall shift the scene from the old Stadacona's heights to the rugged though fertile land to which the magic pencil of Longfellow has lent unfading glamour: to Acadia, now Nova Scotia.

More than one hundred years before the forest primeval and golden wheat-fields of Grand Pré had echoed the sighs of Longfellow's Acadian Maidens. there lived, loved and died on the historic shores of the river St. John, at Fort St. Louis, an accomplished French lady, known to history as the Lady de la Tour.

Claude de St. Etienne, Sieur de la Tour, was allied to the noble French house of Bouillon, but had lost the greater part of his estates in the civil wars. He came to Acadia about the year 1609 with his son Charles, who was then only fifteen years of age.

Charles, after the destruction of Port-Royal by Argall, became the fast friend of Biencourt and lived with him, both leading a free and easy woodman's life. Biencourt claimed important rights in Port-Royal.

At his death, he bequeathed his claims to the young Huguenot, Charles de la Tour, namingh im his lieutenant and successor in the Government of the colony; he could not have selected a bolder, a more enterprising and successful leader.

In 1625, or thereabout, Charles de la Tour married the lady whose adventurous career it is my object to depict.

Shortly after his marriage he removed to a fort he had erected near Cape Sable, which he called Fort St. Louis, and which he also intended to make a convenient depot for Indian trade.

About this period the French colonists were becoming sensible of the weakness of their settlements in Acadia in case of foreign aggression. Claude de la Tour, the father of Charles, was sent to France to represent the matter to the French Government. Returning with ammunition and supplies intended for Port-Royal and Quebec, the squadron, in 1628, was captured with Roquemont's fleet by Sir David Kirk, and Claude de la Tour was sent a prisoner to England. Far from losing heart, he seems to have made the most of his captivity to forward his own ends.

A Huguenot of note, he found favor at once among the French Huguenots who, exiled from their own sunny land by intolerance, had sought an asylum in London.

The English Monarch sought them as useful allies.

Claude de la Tour was introduced to Court, fell in love and married one of the ladies in waiting of Queen Henrietta Maria, the consort of Charles I., and was dubbed a Nova Scotia knight. He, as well as his son who then commanded in Acadia, was promised a grant of 4,500 square miles in the new Scotch colony to be founded there by Sir William Alexander, provided he could persuade his son to hand over his fort to the representatives of the English king.

The unscrupulous parent, on mentioning to his son the price which those flattering distinctions and emoluments were to cost, soon found out that something greater than all they might represent existed, that was summed up in the word "Honor." Charles de la Tour indignantly scorned the parental offer.

Trouble was in store for Charles the moment D'Aulnay

Charnisay, Razely's lieutenant, came to Acadia in command of another settlement. Charnisay was restless, ambitious, revengeful: "Acadia seemed too small for two such aspiring men." Soon Charnisay set to work to supplant his rival at the French Court, and succeeded through powerful friends. The blow fell on De la Tour in 1641; his commission as the King's Lieutenant was revoked and a vessel sailed from France to carry back the deposed Governor. Encouraged by his spirited wife, Charles refused to bend his head to the storm — urging that the King's good faith had been surprised. He fortified the fort, applied to Boston for help and sent a representative to the Huguenots of La Rochelle seeking aid against their great enemy, Richelieu. De Charnisay, in the meantime, had gone over to France to prosecute his deadly plans of revenge against De la Tour, and he heard of the arrival of the Lady De la Tour, whose influence he dreaded very much. He at once procured an order for her arrest, as being an accomplice in her husband's treason. She fled to England and succeeded in chartering a ship in London, which she freighted with provisions and munitions of war to relieve her husband at Fort La Tour. Instead of steering straight for the Fort, the English captain spent several months trading on the coast for his own account. De Charnisay had not remained idle in the meanwhile. On returning he laid watch and succeeded in intercepting the ship; the master had to conceal in the hold his daring passenger, the Lady De la Tour, pretending his vessel was bound for Boston. De Charnisay then gave him a message to deliver to the Boston authorities and he reached there a few days after.

This change of itinerary, added to the untoward delay which had already occurred, was a grievous loss and inconvenience to the Lady De la Tour. She brought suit in Boston against the English captain on the charter-party for damages, which were awarded to her to the extent of £2,000 by a full bench of magistrates. She seized the cargo of the ship and hired three vessels to convey herself and property to Fort La Tour, where she arrived in 1644, to the great joy of her husband, after an absence of more than twelve months.

De Charnisay, after storming at Governor Endicot and the Boston people generally, for having given help to Lady De la Tour, took advantage of the absence of Governor De la Tour from his fort to attack it fiercely, after having first apprised himself of its weak condition. The garrison, 'tis true, was small, but there was at its head an indomitable spirit worth a whole garrison, the Lady De la Tour. She stationed herself on the bastion, directing the cannonade and infusing into the combatants her own heroic spirit. Soon she had the satisfaction of seeing De Charnisay's ship making cover behind a point to prevent her sinking, and twenty of the besiegers laying dead and thirteen wounded. This repulse took place in February, 1645.

De Charnisay's last attack on Fort La Tour occurred on the 13th April, 1645. This time the attack was directed from the land side. Unfortunately, the fort was in no better condition than on former occasions to make an attack; moreover, De la Tour was absent and in Boston, unable to reach the fort, owing to the armed cruisers with which De Charnisay patroled the Bay of Fundy. The Lady De la Tour, though despairing of making a successful resistance, resolved to defend the fort to the last.* For three successive days and nights the storming continued, but the defence was so well managed that the besiegers made no progress and De Charnisay was compelled to retire with loss.

Treachery, however, finally achieved what valor had failed to effect. Charnisay found means to bribe a Swiss sentry who formed part of the garrison, and on the fourth day, an Easter Sunday, while the garrison were at prayers, this traitor permitted the enemy to approach without giving any warning. They were in the act of scaling the walls before the inmates of the fort were aware of their attack. Lady De la Tour instantly rushed out at the head of her soldiers and fought the besiegers with so much vigor that Charnisay, who had already lost twelve men besides many wounded, despaired of the success of his undertaking. He therefore proposed terms of capitulation, offering the garrison life and liberty if they consented to surrender. Lady De la Tour, persuaded that successful resistance was no longer possible and desirous of saving the lives of those under her command, accepted the terms offered by Charnisay and allowed him to enter the fort....

It was then that the full baseness of Charnisay's nature was revealed. With the exception of one man, he ordered the

---

* Madame De la Tour's career is the subject of one of John Greenleaf Whittier's sweetest poems, entitled: *Saint John, 1647*. The noble conduct of her husband in refusing to surrender to his father's sollicitations, for the English king, the French fort he held, was immortalized in verse by the late Gérin-Lajoie, one of our leading writers, in a drama, entitled: *Le Jeune Latour*.

whole garrison, French as well as English, to be hanged; the one life he spared was on the dreadful condition that he should become the executioner of his comrades in arms. Even the slaughter of these poor soldiers failed to satisfy his bloodthirsty instincts. Had he dared, he would doubtless have had Lady De la Tour assassinated with the rest; but the Court of France, venal though it was, might not have tolerated such an outrage. Charnisay did what was almost as contemptible; the heroic woman, with a rope around her neck, like one who should also have been executed, but who by favor had been reprieved, was forced to be present at the execution of her soldiers. It mattered nought to her what further schemes of vengeance her implacable foe might devise. None could move her, her great heart was broken. She was far away from her husband, to whose fortunes she had been so faithful; she dared scarcely hope to see his face again, except, like herself, a captive. Her work in life was done; she felt she was not born for captivity, so she faded away and drooped day by day, until her heroic soul left its earthy tenement. Within three weeks after the capture of the fort she was laid to rest on the green banks of the St. Johns River, which she had loved so well, and where she had lived for so many years, "leaving a name as proudly enshrined in Acadian history," says the historian, "as that of any sceptered Queen in European history."

Let us now review one of those energetic characters which marked one of the proudest epochs in Canadian history: The era of Frontenac.

You have all heard of the dashing French regiment of Carignan, commanded by Colonel de Salières, which the Grand

Monarque, Louis XIV., in 1664, had given his haughty Vice-Roy, the Marquis de Tracy, as an escort to Quebec. It was officered by sixty or seventy French gentlemen, many of whom were connected with the French noblesse. Four companies, some six hundred men, were disbanded shortly after their arrival in New France. The officers and privates were induced, by land grants, supplies of cattle and other marks of royal favor to marry and settle in the New World. Many of them acquiesced and became the respected sires of the leading French families in after years. Among them De Chambly, Sorel, Du Gué, La Valtrie, Verchères, Berthier, Granville, Contrecœur, De Meloises, Tarieu de la Pérade, Saint-Ours, De la Fouille, Maximin, Lobeau, Petit, Rougemont, Traversy, De la Nouette, Lacombe and others, worthy comrades in arms of De Longueuil, d'Iberville, and de Ste-Hélène.

One of them, M. de Verchères, obtained in 1672, on the banks of the St. Lawrence, near Montreal, where now stands the flourishing parish of Verchères, a land-grant, of three miles square, which the King materially increased in extent the following year.

In those troublesome times, the seigneur's house meant a small fort, to stave off Indian aggression. "These forts," says the historian Charlevoix, "were merely extensive enclosures, surrounded by palisades and redoubts. The church and the dwelling of the seigneur were within the enclosure, which was sufficiently large to admit, on an emergency, the women and children, and the farm-cattle; one or two sentries mounted guard by day and by night; with small field pieces, they kept in check the skulking enemy and served to warn the settlers to arm and hasten to the rescue. These precautions were sufficient to guard against a raid," but not in all cases as we shall soon see.

Taking advantage of the absence of M. de Verchères, the ever-watchful Iroquois drew stealthily around the little fort and took to climbing over the palisades. On hearing which, Marie-Madeleine de Verchères, the youthful daughter of the seigneur, seized a musket and fired it. The marauders alarmed, slunk away, but on finding that they were not pursued, they returned and spent two days hovering like wolves around the fort, however not daring to enter, as ever and anon a bullet would reach the man who first attempted an escalade. What increased their surprise, was that they could detect inside no living creature except a woman; but this female was so active, so fearless, so ubiquitous, that she seemed to be everywhere at once. Nor did her unerring fire cease, so long as there was an enemy in sight. The dauntless holder of the fort Verchères was Mlle de Verchères, then in her twelfth year. This happened in 1690.

Two years later, the Iroquois returned in larger force, having chosen the time of the year when the settlers were engaged in the fields, tilling the soil, to pounce upon them. Mlle de Verchères, then aged fourteen, happened to be sauntering on the river bank. Noticing a savage aiming at her, she eluded his murderous intent by rushing homeward at the top of her speed; but for swiftness of foot the Indian was her match, terror added wings to her flight. With tomahawk upraised, he gradually gained upon her, and was in fact rapidly closing as they neared the fort, another bound and she might be beyond his reach. Straining every nerve, the Indian sprang and seized the kerchief which covered her throat. Rapid as thought, and whilst the exulting savage raised his arm to strike the fatal blow, Mademoiselle tore asunder the knot which fastened her kerchief, and, bounding within the fort like a gazelle, closed the door against her pursuer.

"To arms! To arms!!" Without heeding the groans of the inmates, who could see from the fort their husbands and brothers carried away as prisoners, she rushed to the bastion, where stood the solitary sentry, seized a musket and a soldier's cap, and ordered a great clatter of guns, so as to make believe the fort was fully manned. She next loaded a small field-piece, and not having a wad at hand, thrust in a towel instead, and discharged the piece at the enemy. This unexpected rebuff, struck terror in the marauders, who saw their warriors one after the other grievously hit. Thus armed and with but the aid of one soldier only, she continued the fire. Presently the alarm reached the neighborhood of Montreal, when an intrepid officer, the Chevalier de Crisasi, brother to the Marquis of Crisasi, then Governor of Three Rivers, rushed to Verchères at the head of a chosen band of men; but the savages had made good their retreat with three prisoners. After a three days pursuit, the Chevalier found them with their captives strongly intrenched in the woods on the borders of Lake Champlain. The French officer completely routed the murderous crew—cut them to pieces only a few who escaped. The prisoners were released, all New France resounded with the fame of Mlle de Verchères who was awarded the title of heroine.

Another instance of heroism on her part, added fame to her

reputation for courage. A French commander, M. de La Naudière de la Pérade, was pursuing the Iroquois, some writers say in the neighborhood of the river Richelieu, according to others in the vicinity of the river Ste.-Anne, when there sprang, unexpectedly, out of the underbrush, a swarm of the implacable foes. Taken unaware M. de la Pérade was just on the point of falling a victim to their ambush when Mlle de Verchères, seizing a musket, rushed on the enemy at the head of some resolute men and succeeded in saving him from the Indian tomahawk. She had achieved a conquest, or better she became the conquest of M. de la Pérade, whose life she saved. Henceforth, in history, the heroine de Verchères will be known as Madame de la Pérade, the wife of an influential seigneur.

The fame of the heroine reached the banks of the Seine, and Louis XIV. instructed his Vice-Roy in New France to call upon her in person and procure her version of her courageous deeds. The simple statement pleased the French Monarch very much.

It was my intention to close the career of the Heroine of Verchères with this last episode, but on the eve of my leaving for New York, an antiquarian friend, a lineal descendant also of this noble woman, the Hon. Justice George Baby, of the Court of Appeals, placed in my hand an unpublished memoir revealing Madame de la Pérade, as possessing the uncommon courage and presence of mind you have just admired, not merely in the spring-tide of her existence, but retaining it as well in the autumn of life.

This document, aside of its historical value, gives interesting glimpses of the vicissitudes of the daily life of the Canadian seigneurs in those time. Possibly you will forgive me for trespassing on your indulgence a few moments longer, to give you in English a few extracts. "Many years," says the Memoir,* "after Mlle de Verchères' marriage to M. Tarieu de la Naudière, Sieur de la Pérade, she was instrumental in saving his life a second time. The Iroquois, true to their sanguinary instincts and to their deadly hatred of the French, never paddled past Ste.-Anne de la Pérade without leaving there some trace of their hatred. About sunset, one mellow September afternoon, either believing that M. de la Pérade was absent and that they had a chance to surprise the settlement, they landed. The seignorial manor stood apart from other dwellings, a short distance from the river, secluded from public gaze by a thick growth of forest trees. Madame de la Pérade's aged husband was confined to his bed grievously ill. Except his wife and a young maid servant sixteen years of age, no other inmates were inside.

"The marauding Indians suddenly, landed from their canoes which the rushes hid from view. One party marched

* This narrative, adds Judge Baby, I had from my aged aunt, Mlle Marguerite de La Naudière, a granddaughter of the heroine, who expired at Quebec on the 17th of November, 1856, at the age of 81 years.

The venerable Mlle de La Naudière was for years in Quebec a kind of landmark between the past and the present. Her memory, conversational powers and repartees, made her sought after by the highest in the land; her dignified and courteous manners reminded one of the old school. More than once our Governors General and their families called on her, in her St.-Louis Street mansion; among others, the Earl of Elgin, Sir Edmund Walker Head, Lord Monck. After his departure, Lord Elgin, kept up with her a friendly correspondence until her death.

towards the house, whilst another crouched behind the trees waiting for a signal.

"A glimpse at the savages revealed to Madame de la Pérade what fate awaited her and her husband. She forthwith bolted and barricaded the front door as best she could, coolly directing her maid to fetch the only two fire-arms left by the absent farm hands, she determined to face the foe, and if possible keep them outside.

"The leader of the band and his blood-thirsty crew, had scarcely ascended the wide flight of steps which led to the front door of the manor, when she, without even allowing him to speak, addressed him in his own dialect and in a firm voice asked what he wanted.

"The chief, taken aback at hearing a white woman speak his language, replied, in a subdued tone, that he wished to confer with M. de la Pérade—that he was the bearer of an important message, stating that he and his friends knew enough of the hospitality of M. de la Pérade to warrant their visit to his house and to expect meat and drink as well; that they were hungry and thirsty, adding also that a little fire-water would be acceptable.

"Madame de la Pérade, without exhibiting the slightest fear, replied that her husband was engaged, could not see them told them to leave.

"The chief, convinced that he had merely to deal with a lone woman, exchanged in a whisper a few words with his followers; then, raising his tone, insolently answered that if the door was not instantly thrown open, that they would soon find a way to enter.

"Well did Madame de la Pérade know the treatment which

awaited her, should the Indians enter. Her husband lay helplessly ill, within hearing of all this. Something had to be done, and that instantly. Sending up to heaven a prayer for help, she felt stronger, and, undaunted, spoke as follows: 'The door shall remain closed, and if you refuse to go, I shall find means to compel you.'

"The savages used their utmost strength in order to break in; in those days the door of a Canadian manor required to be strong, as you may be sure.

"Baffled, the Indians rushed down the steps, uttering their terrible war-whoop. Then crowding abreast a window, through which they felt sure to find a passage, they poured in a volley of shot and bullets which went crashing through the sash and lodged in the wainscot and rafters.

"Quick as lightning, Madame de la Pérade fired on the murderous redskins, first one gun, then another. Astonished by this vigorous reception, the marauders wavered, shrank back, and finally retreated bearing one of their comrades wounded in the leg. Instantly reloading, Madame de la Pérade, had just time, under the gathering shadows of evening, to give the retreating horde another volley. One of those panics common to Indians seems to have occurred; and fancying the place was protected they ran to their canoes.

"The brave woman's trials were only half over, for at this moment, her young maid came rushing to her, saying: 'The roof is on fire!' Parthian like, in their retreat, the Iroquois, had directed flaming arrows towards the old peaked moss-covered gable. How could her sick husband escape the flames? Even if she should succeed in carrying him beyond their reach, were not the Indians lurking in the neighboring woods and watching for a chance to pounce upon them?

"She was not yet aware that the defeated savages were retreating in their canoes from an imaginary pursuing foe. Her first impulse was to ascend to the burning roof with her maid and pour water on the flames; her next thought was to rush through the smoke and fire to the apartment where M. de la Pérade lay, and implore him to rise and save himself. But all in vain, he was too enfeebled. Thanking his devoted wife, he replied that it seemed as if it were the will of God he should die then. 'Adieu! Adieu! my kind and true friend,' said he, 'twice under God's dispensation your heroism has saved me from the Indian tomahawk. To-day, God calls me! I am ready. Adieu.'

"Madame de la Pérade, momentarily crushed by this harrowing scene, suddenly felt herself endowed with a supernatural fortitude, and, seizing her sick husband in her arms she carried him out, deposited him on the grass, and then, physically and mentally exhausted fell insensible by his side.

"The evening was calm and the fire smouldered slowly on the house-top. Soon a shower which had been threatening, broke, and in a measure put out the fire whose reflection had attracted the tenantry who came to the rescue."

The heroine of Verchères expired at Ste.-Anne, on the 7th August, 1737.

Have these remarkable careers no lessons? In Madame de Champlain, we have a lady of noble birth, youth and beauty; a life pure and gentle, and kindliness combined to such a degree as to make the possessor appear "more than human" to those among whom fate had cast her.

Madame de la Tour exhibits a sterner, more Spartan spirit, ready at all times to confront war contumely, adversity in its direst form; a model of sweet, womanly devotion to her husband and of self-sacrifice to duty.

In Mlle de Verchères, you have to admire the warm blood of youth blending with the cool courage of maturer years; the masculine daring of the sterner portion of humanity pulsating through a heart of fourteen summers, and gathering strength with the weight of years.

Allow me to close my remarks with the sentiment expressed in my opening: May Providence, in its clemency, continue to send us more of those true, tender and brave spirits, beacons from on high, to light up the rugged path of erring, mortal man!

Works on Canadian History consulted :—

Histoire de la Colonie Française en Canada.—FAILLOU, Vol. I, pp. 17, 185, 252.

Cours d'Histoire du Canada.—FERLAND, Vol. I, p. 234.

First Conquest of Canada.—KIRKE, p. 69.

Relations des Jésuites.

Chroniques des Ursulines de Meaux.—JOURNAL DE QUÉBEC, 1854.

History of Nova Scotia.—Beamish Murdoch.

History of Acadia.—J. Cavenay.

Histoire des Grandes Familles Françaises du Canada.—Daniel.

Histoire du Canada.—Charlevoix, Vol. III, pp. 124, 125.

Histoire du Canada.—Bibaud *père.*

Panthéon Canadien.—Bibaud *jeune,* p. 295.

Histoire de l'Amérique Septentrionale.—Baqueville de la Potherne.

Mémoires et Lettres de famille.—Hon. Judge Geo. Baby.

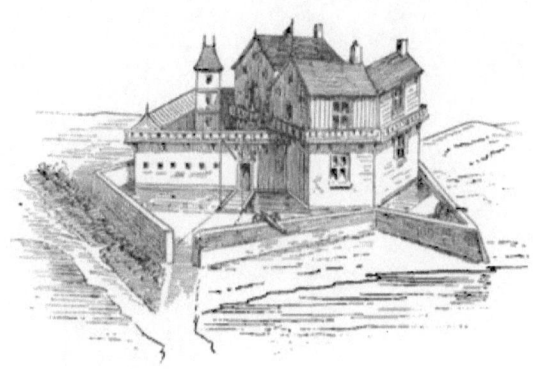

127[1]

LITERATURE IN CANADA.

BY
GEO. STEWART, Jr.,
D. C. L., F. R. G. S., F. R. S. C.

Read before the Canadian Club of New York.

EING deeply sensible of the honor which the Canadian Club has paid me this evening, in asking me to be its guest, I beg of you to accept in return my heart-felt thanks. I thank you also for the very flattering invitation which has been given me to address you on a subject, in which all Canadians must, I am sure, take a warm and appreciative interest. To have my name inscribed on your list of guests, is an honor which I need not assure you, I value most highly. The Canadian Club of New York,

is an institution of which we Canadians feel justly proud, because we know that it is a credit to our countrymen in every way, that it is continually extending and broadening its influence and importance, and that its roll of membership represents all that is best in the political, social and commercial activity of Canada's sons in the great American metropolis. But admirable as its character for hospitality unquestionably is, the Club is more than a means for supplying a place of pleasant resort for resident and visiting Canadians in New York. It is an educator, in a certain sense, and the present series of literary and social entertainments, will do much to stimulate Canadian sentiment, patriotism and aspiration. The pleasure of these meetings too, is materially heightened by the happy manner in which your Committee considers the claims of that element in our population which is always fair and gentle, and to whose refining influences the sterner sex owes so much. With such sharers of your exile from your native land, as I see before me to-night, radiant and charming as they all are, I am forced to the conclusion that your self-imposed banishment cannot be so very hard to bear after all. You do right, Mr. President, in opening your splendid rooms to the ladies on occasions like the present one, and it is an example which I think ought to be followed, and no doubt will be, by other clubs.

But, you have asked me to address you a few words on the subject of literature in Canada. As you are aware, ladies and gentlemen, Canadian authorship is still in its infancy. The plough has proved a mightier engine than the pen, and authorship has been followed feebly and precariously by men and women, who have never lost heart in their work, but whose labors have been rewarded in too many instances, I fear, by those soft words, which, however sweet to the ear, fail entirely to butter our parsnips. No one has been able, in Canada, to make the writing of books his sole means of living. We have had to write our books under our breath, as it may be said, and the marvel is that we have been able to produce, under such depressing circumstances, so many works of even respectable merit. The Canadian author is either a professional or a business man, and his literary work must be done, almost as an accomplishment, during the leisure moments which may be snatched from the exacting occupations of real life. Of course, authorship prosecuted under such disadvantages, must suffer, but notwithstanding many drawbacks, the mental output of the Dominion is not inconsiderable. At the recent Indian and Colonial Exhibition, in London, no fewer than 3,000 volumes, all by native authors, were shown in the library of the Canadian section, and this exhibit, as you know, by no means exhausts the list of books actually written by Canadians, during a century of time. The collection represented Canadian authorship in every department of its literature, science, history and poetry being especially large and noteworthy, while the other branches were not neglected.

Territorially, our country is extensive, and our literary sons and daughters are to be encountered, now, from British Columbia to Cape Breton, doing work which is good, and some of it destined to stand. Fréchette, the laureate of the French Academy, not long ago, said, " Be Canadians and the future is yours." " That which strikes us most in your poems," said one of the Forty Immortals to the poet, "is that the modern style, the Parisian style of your verses is united to something strange, so particular and singular it seems an exotic, disengaged from the entire work." This perfume of originality which this author discovered was at that time unknown to Fréchette. What was it? It was the secret of their nationality, the certificate of their origin, their Canadian stamp. And it is important never to allow this character to disappear. There is much in this. Our country is full of history, full of character, full of something to be met with nowhere else in the world. A mine of literary wealth is to be had in every section of the dominion, and it only awaits the hand of the craftsman. Bret Harte opened up a new phase of American character as he discovered it in wild California. Miss Murfree found the Tennessee mountains rich in incident and strong in episodes of an intensely dramatic color, and Mr. Cable developed in a brilliant and picturesque way life and movement among the Creoles of the South. Have we no Canadian authors among us, who can do as much for us? Lespérance, it is true, has dealt with one period of our history, in a captivating way. Kirby has told the story of "The Golden Dog" with fine and alert sympathies. Miss Macfarlane's "Children of the Earth" depends on Nova Scotia for its scenic effects. Marmette has presented, with some power, half a dozen romances of the French régime, while Fréchette has dramatized the story of Papineau's rebellion.

But Canada is full of incident and romance, and the poet and novelist have fruitful themes enough on which to build many a fanciful poem and story. In history, we have much good writing, and I trust you will permit me to say, that I think our young historians would do well not to attempt to do too much. I would advise them to deal with periods rather than to write complete histories of the whole country. Mr. John Charles Dent has been most successful on two occasions, giving us the history of old Canada, from the Union of 1841 to the present time, and following up his labors with the "Story of the Upper Canadian Rebellion." Mr. Edmund Collins has written of Canada under Lord Lorne's administration, and in the *Life and Times of Sir John A. Macdonald* he has discussed, with considerable independence, Canada's political and economical progress during a burning period of our history. The Abbés Casgrain and Faillon, Judge Gray, Mr. Globensky, Mr. Turcotte, Mr. George E. Fenety and Mr. de Gaspé have also dealt with epochs, and so have Messrs. David, Carrier, Bryce and Adam.

In works relating to parliamentary procedure and practice, we have the notable contributions of Alpheus Todd, John George Bourinot and Joseph Doutre. And in books of purely antiquarian character, we have the investigations of Scadding, Hawkins, Lemoine and Lawrence, while our annals, from day to day, have found an industrious exponent in Mr. Henry J. Morgan. Our larger historians are chiefly Ferland, Faillon, Garneau, Withrow, Campbell, Sulte, Beamish Murdoch and McMullen. In biography we have the names of Fennings Taylor, Alexander MacKenzie, Charles Lindsey, P. B. Casgrain and William Rattray. In poetry we have a good showing, but I need scarcely name more than Reade, Roberts, Mair, Murray, Heavysege, Miss Machar, Mrs. Harrison ("Seranus") among the English; and Crémazie, Fréchette, Le May, Legendre and Routhier among the French. The list would not be complete were I to omit a few of our essayists and writers on special topics, such as Col. G. T. Denison, whose history of Cavalry won the great Russian prize, Principal Grant, Chauveau, Le Sueur, Samuel Dawson, Oxley, Jack, Griffin, Ellis, Faucher de St. Maurice, Harper and George Murray. To studies on political economy and finance we have contributed no prominent names as writers of treatises on those subjects, but George Hague and the late Charles F. Smithers of Montreal have presented the banking side of the argument, in sound, practical papers of great value. In almost every department of scientific investigation and thought we have an array of men of whom any country might be proud, some of them having a fame which is world-wide. Briefly, I may mention a few of these, such as the Dawsons, father and son, Drs. Wilson, Hunt, Hamel, Selwyn, Bell, Laflamme, Lawson, MacGregor, Bailey, and Messrs. Sandford Fleming, Matthews, Murdoch, Carpmael, Johnson, Hoffman, Bayne and Macfarlane. Of course, this list, by no means, includes all.

The education of the French Canadian is much more literary than scientific. His taste for letters is cultivated at quite an early age, and oratory, *belles-lettres* and the classics form by far the stronger part of his mental outfit on leaving college. Higher thought and scientific research have few charms for him which he cannot withstand, and he turns, with passion almost, to poetry, romance, light philosophy and history. He is an insatiable reader, but his taste is circumscribed and narrowed, and following the bent of his inclinations, he eschews all the troublesome paradoxes of literature, avoids speculative authors, and reads with delight and appreciation the books which furnish him with the most amusement. He seeks recreation in his reading matter, and, sympathizing with Emerson, though he scarcely knows a line of that author, he makes it a point to read only the books which please him the best. He likes clever verses and a good novel, and as the printing-press of France furnishes exemplars of these in abundance, he is never put to straits for supplies. Naturally enough, when the French Canadian attempts authorship, he writes poetry, romances, *chroniques* and history. The latter he does very well, and exhibits industry and skill in the arrangement of his materials and the grouping of his facts. His work rarely fails in artistic merit, and its strength lies in the easy flow and elegance of its diction, and the spirit in which the author approaches his subject. Quebec's list of poets is a long one. Almost every fairly-educated young man can, at will, produce a copy of well-turned verse, but fortunately all do not exercise their power, nor do those who print poems in the newspapers always make volumes of their lays afterwards. Strange to say, Quebec is singularly badly-off for female poets. I know of but one or two ladies who have courted the muses and printed their verses. We must not forget, however, that a poem is often emphasized in the tying of a ribbon, in the arrangement of the hair, and in the fashioning of a bow, and it would be unfair to describe Quebec's young women as unpoetical merely because they have not seen fit to put their thoughts into song. There are many male poets in the province, but it will be unnecessary to concern ourselves, at this time, with more than half a dozen of the better-known ones. These are Crémazie, Fréchette, Le May, Garneau, Routhier and Sulte, each distinct from the other, in style, touch and motive. Joseph Octave Crémazie deserves, perhaps, the special title of national poet of French Canada, but Louis Honoré Fréchette, whose versatility and fancy rise to great heights, is not far below him. There are few prominent novelists, as I have said, of either French or English origin. The name of James de Mille, a New-Brunswicker, stands out prominently, but his fiction is little tinctured with the Canadian flavor. Among the French, we have only Chauveau, Marmette, Bourassa and Le May.

Literature in Canada, owes much to the various literary and historial societies, which exist in nearly all the chief towns of the Dominion. The parent of them all is the old Literary and Historical Society of Quebec, which was founded in 1824, by the Earl of Dalhousie, then Governor-General. This institution owns many rare manuscripts and printed books, relating to the early history of the country, and every year its treasures are explored and investigated by historians and enquirers from all parts of the Continent. The Society has published some valuable memoirs, transactions and manuscripts in French and in English, and these are held in high repute by scholars everywhere. In Montreal, Toronto, Halifax, St. John, N. B., and Winnipeg, similar societies enjoy a flourishing and useful existence. Four years ago, the Marquis of Lorne, founded the Royal Society of Canada. The membership was limited to eighty men, and the objects of the society may be thus described : firstly, to encourage studies and investigations in literature and science; secondly, to publish transactions containing the minutes of proceedings at meetings, records of the work performed, original papers and memoirs of merit, and such other documents as might be deemed worthy of publication; thirdly, to offer prizes or other inducements for valuable papers on subjects relating to Canada, and to aid researches already begun and carried so far as to render their ultimate value probable; fourthly, to assist in the collection of specimens, with a view to the formation of a Canadian Museum of Archives, Ethnology, Archæology and Natural History. The society is divided into four sections; 1.—French Literature, with history, archæology and allied subjects; 2.—English Literature with history, archæology and allied subjects; 3.—Mathematical, chemical and physical sciences; 4.—Geological and biological sciences. The sections meet separately for the reading and discussion of papers, or other business, during the annual session of the society, which has so far assembled at Ottawa in the month of May. These meetings have been most successful, in point of attendance and work actually performed, and the usefulness of the society has been greatly extended by its catholicity and liberality towards kindred institutions, almost every one of which, in Canada, has been invited annually to send delegates to the Royal. These representatives have the privilege of taking part in all general or sectional meetings for reading and discussing papers. They may also communicate a statement of original work done, and papers published during the year by their own societies, and may report on any matters which the Royal Society may usefully aid in publication or otherwise. The

Dominion Government aids the Royal Society by an annual grant of $5,000, which is set aside for the publication of the transactions and proceedings. Thus far, four large volumes have been published, and a glance at their contents affords convincing testimony of the value of the work which the society is doing. Its weak point, doubtless, rests in the literary sections. But even those departments may be made valuable and eminently useful in time. In archæology, history and ethnology the field is wide, and it is satisfactory to note that the two first sections are already devoting their energies to their special line of work with vigor and zeal. In one branch of study, in particular, that of ethnology, the Royal Society has an important duty to perform. The Indian population is fast disappearing. In a few years, the characteristics of the red races will be wholly lost. It is necessary to preserve these, while the tribes remain, and this work is being done by the second section of the Royal Society, and it is a work which possesses a value that cannot be over estimated. Of course, in historical research, and in archæological investigation, the extent of the society's labors is practically unlimited. Royal societies, with similar objects in view, exist in various quarters of the globe. Canada surely, is old enough and advanced enough to have one also.

In a paper such as this, some reference should be made to the really admirable Department of Archives, which is maintained by the Dominion Government at Ottawa. It is under the charge of that competent and zealous officer, Mr. Douglas Brymner, whose tastes and training well fit him for the duties of his office. He has really created the department and made it one of the most efficient in the public service of Canada.

Fifteen years ago the historical records of Canada had scarcely an abiding place. We had no regular system by which letters, pamphlets, printed books and documents and manuscripts relating to the commercial, literary and political activity of the country could be preserved, and rendered accessible to the student. Thousands of valuable papers were in imminent danger of being lost ; many undoubtedly did perish. In 1871, a number of literary men of Canada, petitioned the legislature to organize a branch of the public service by means of which historical data might be preserved. Parliament promptly acceded to this request, and the Minister of Agriculture added the Archives branch to his department. Mr. Brymner was placed in charge, and he began his work of collecting absolutely *ab ovo*, not a single document of any sort being in hand when he commenced. To-day, the shelves of the Department contain upwards of seven thousand volumes of historical papers on every conceivable subject of interest to Canadians. The work of indexing these enormous collections goes on daily, and fresh matter is constantly being added, Mr. Brymner's aim being to make the Archives truly national in every respect and as complete as possible.

Much has been written about the law of copyright. Canada passed a fairly good act in 1875, but as it contravened the Imperial statute, it was not long before the authorities in London declared the act *ultra vires*, and our publishers have been in a most unhappy frame of mind ever since. In a word, the business of publishing books in Canada is at a pretty low ebb, and publishers find little encouragement in extending their trade. The Canadian author is not so badly off, just now.

Under the old British act, a very good rule only worked one way. Thus, the English author who copyrighted his book in England was fully protected in every colony flying the British flag. The Canadian or Australian author, however, could only obtain copyright in the colony or province where his book was published. The other day, an amendment was made to the act by the Imperial Parliament, and by its terms, any work published in the Queen's dominions is fully protected all over the vast empire. The various colonial governments were communicated with on the subject, and all but New South Wales replied favorably. That far-off dependency remains to be heard from. Meanwhile, the act was passed, and for the benefit of New South Wales a clause was inserted exempting any colony from the operation of the measure, should it prefer to keep to the old order of things.

And, just here, is a good place to ask, do Canadians read the productions of their own authors? What encouragement do they give the writers of Canadian books? It is a fact that Canada cannot support a really first-class magazine. The experiment of magazine publishing has been tried in all the chief cities of the Dominion, but it has failed in every instance, though the trial has been made honestly and at considerable sacrifice on the part of the promoters of the enterprise. Every now and then we hear the question: Why does Canada not have a magazine? The Canadians read magazines, and pay for them. This is true; but it is also true that they want the best. Their standard is high, and unless the publisher can supply a publication which can compete with the important old world and United States serials, they will not have it, no matter how patriotic they may suppose themselves to be. Of course, the day is coming when Canada will have its great monthly and still greater quarterly, but the time is not yet ripe. In the meantime, the question which presses for solution is, what are we doing, in a helpful way, for our own authors in the Dominion? Are we encouraging them to write and publish? We know that men like Dr. Daniel Wilson, Prof. Clark Murray and Mr. Grant Allen, and some others who could be named, never think of publishing their books in Canada. They have something to say, and expression to their views is always given in the largest possible field. They find it to their advantage to publish in England or in the United States. Small editions of their books are sometimes sold to Canadian booksellers, either in sheets, or bound up within cloth covers, but the copies so disposed of, yield scarcely a tithe of the remuneration which reaches the successful author, from the sale of his books in the great markets in which they first see the light. The Canadian author cannot be blamed for making the most of his opportunities, in this way. The market in Canada is limited, and, as a general thing, if a Canadian book is published in Canada, little can be realized out of the venture. There are exceptions to every rule of course, and a few Canadian books, written and published in the Dominion, have repaid their authors very well. Mr. Dent's *Last Forty Years* and his *Story of the Upper Canadian Rebellion*, Principal Grant's *Ocean to Ocean*, Mr. Bourinot's book on Parliamentary Practice, *Picturesque Canada*, Mr. Bengough's amusing *Caricature History of Canadian Politics*, Mr. Lemoine's historical sketches, and perhaps, half a dozen other books, have yielded handsome returns to their authors, but the great majority of our Canadian books have hardly paid the publisher in his outlay for printing and binding. Mr. John Lovell, whose experience in the business of book-publishing has been varied and extensive, used to call the fruits of his enterprise, his "housekeepers." Eventually, thousands of these volumes found their way to the trunk-makers and the auction shops. And the same thing is still going on. Now what can be said on the subject? We cannot force the public of Canada to buy and read the works of Canadian writers. Our people are a reading community, and judging from the collection of books which may be seen in most houses, their literary taste is good. It might be said that Canadian books are not bought because the style of their authors is not of the highest excellence, that crudity and not elegance is their chief characteristic, and that in point of topic and treatment they possess little that is calculated to commend them to the book-buyer. But is this true?

We often speak of Canadian literature, but let us ask ourselves the question: Have we a literature of our own? Certainly, we have writers of books; but does the literary work which they perform constitute a literature, in the fullest meaning of the term? Mr. Charles Dudley Warner has voiced the idea that the lack of intellectual activity of the Canadians is due to the fact that they have to put forth so much of their physical energy in an endeavor to keep warm. But Mr. Warner's delicious satire is often extravagant, we know, and we also know that he is never quite so extravagant as when he undertakes to deal with Canadian affairs. Mr. Carter Troop, the other day, discussed Mr. Warner's views, in some sharp paragraphs, in the New York *Critic ;* but, at the same time, he felt constrained to acknowledge that in Canada there was considerable "literary feebleness." The cause of this he ascribes to our "humble political status." "As a colony," he writes, "Canada possesses neither the higher attributes nor the graver responsibilities of national existence ; and where such attributes and responsibilities are wanting, national life and feeling, the source and inspiration of all literary achievements, will be equally wanting." Of course, this simply means that the colonial position is fatal to the development of our higher intellectual life and movement,—literary genius in fact,—and that the panacea for our ills in that respect is independence alone. I cannot go as far as that, though I must admit that the idea is suggestive and may be discussed. American letters, we know, during the colonial period, were feeble and insignificant. After years of independence came a literature, full of promise and character. But has its present robust condition been reached by independence merely? Must Canada pursue a similar course of political advancement, if she would have a literature of marked individuality, color and strength? I should be sorry to think so. Canada is still young in years, and time will work a change. American literature has grown with the increase in the ranks of the leisure class in the United States, and education has done the rest. Only a few decades ago, the people of the great Republic, were largely dependent on British and European authors for their intellectual food. Even the serials in the leading magazines of New York, Boston and Philadelphia, were from the pens of English novelists. The literature which we all admire to-day, is really almost of yesterday. Most of us can remember when America had hardly more than three or four fiction writers of repute, while half a dozen gentlemen only were writing the ballads and poems of the nation, and of the half-dozen, not more than four were distinctively American in their treatment of scenery and incident. Give Canada a chance. Give her time to have a large leisure class. Give to her literary men and women, the incentive and encouragement they need, and Canadian authorship will not lack in individuality and robustness. Much has been done in the way of education. Our wealthy men are endowing colleges, and founding scholarships in the universities. Our schools are practically free; in some of our provinces, they are entirely free. Perhaps, we are crowding too many men into the professions, but in time, even this error, if it be an error, will regulate itself. The country is beginning to pay attention to what men of culture and of thought have to say about the various problems of life and of human experience. Our lectures attract larger and more appreciative audiences. The people read more, and they are exercising greater discrimination in their reading than they ever did before, and, from all these signs, I feel that I am safe in predicting that the day of successful Canadian authorship is not far distant, and that we will yet have a literature of which we may feel reasonably proud, and that too, without changing our allegiance or altering our system of political and national life.

1441

ECHOES FROM OLD ACADIA.

BY
Prof. CHAS. G. D. ROBERTS,
Kings College, Windsor, N. S.

Read before the Canadian Club of New York.

THE LIFTING OF THE CURTAIN.

ART of the making of our beloved maple-leaf land has been played by the seaward sister province which once together formed Acadia. Walled round with fogs, and rocks and inhospitable seas, Acadia, now divided into New Brunswick and Nova Scotia, is lovely at heart with sunshine and fertility. Her harbors are gateways leading from a region of storm and wild tides into a land of delicious summers, a land of tumbling streams and blue lakes, of ample meadows deep with grass and flowers drowsing through the long afternoons, of vast forests so thick that their grim shadows know scarcely touch of sun. And one of these well favored Acadian havens lured to itself the first settlement that struck root in the whole broad country, now called Canada. This was the harbor of Port Royal, wherein de Monts set a colony in 1605.

It was seventy years before this that a drama had been opened upon the Acadian stage. On the 30th of June, 1534, it began, when Cartier sighted Cape Escuminac (locally now Skiminac), on the gulf shore of New Brunswick.

Coming from the bleak, forbidding coasts of Newfoundland, which he deemed to be Cain's portion of the earth, the harshest corner of Acadia appeared to Cartier a Paradise. The wide water in which he found himself was Miramichi Bay. Not discovering the Miramichi itself, whose mouth lay hidden close at hand, behind long ranges of sand pits, chains of islands, and intricate shoals, he landed on the banks of a lesser river, not identified among the thousand that overlace that region with their silver courses. This stream rippled shallow over its gleaming pebbles, and swarmed with trout and salmon. The wide woods about were of pine and cedar, elm and oak, birch, willow, fir, maple and tamarack, and the sailor's hearts rejoiced over such unlimited possibilities of ships. Where the woods gave back a little space, the ground was covered with wild fruits. Great melting strawberries betrayed themselves by their red gleams piercing the matted grass. The bronze-green blackberry thickets were heavy with their yet unripened fruitage, and the wild pea trammelled his footsteps with its ropes of purple and pale green. This prodigal land was populous with game. When wild pigeons in innumerable flocks streamed past and darkened the air, the heavens seemed as thick with wings as the sea and streams with the countless salmon passing the shoals. Every sedge-grown marsh was noisy with ducks. Plover and curlew piped clearly about the edges of the pools. And the people possessing this land were friendly and few.

Bearing northward, Cartier's weather-darkened sails were soon wafting him over the fairest bay his eyes had yet rested upon. Its waters were clear green, and scarce rippled under the steep sun of mid-July. No reefs, no shoals, but here and there a dark green island asleep on the sleepy tide. On either hand a long receding line of lofty shores drawing close together towards the west, and shading gently from indigo to pale violet. So great was the change from the raw winds of the gulf to this sultry sea that Cartier named it Baie des Chaleurs. Here they passed some days very sweetly in indolent exploration, in trading with the hospitable Micmacs, in feasting on seal flesh and salmon. So commercial were the natives of this land that they bartered the clothes they wore for trades and trinkets. Then Cartier sailed on to the north, to discover the St. Lawrence. And the picture of this visit of his to Acadian shores is the mere fleeting revelation of a lightening in the night, with thicker darkness following after it.

AT THE ST. CROIX MOUTH.

After a lapse of nearly three-quarters of a century, Acadian history makes a real beginning at the St. Croix mouth. To the Sieur de Monts were given letters patent, conferring on him the title of Lieutenant-General of the Territory of Acadia, with full power, between the 40th and 46th parallels, to divide and bestow the land as he might see fit; with power also of monopolizing trade, of making war and peace, and ordinances and law. With him set sail from Hâvre de Grace, in March 1604, Baron de Poutrincourt, and the father of Canada, Champlain. In June the prospective colony, in search of an abiding place, having rejected Port Rossignol and the pastoral valley of Port Royal, having traversed the yellow turbulence of the Bay of Fundy and discovered the rock-bastioned harbor hollowed by the outflow of the St. John, found itself among the myriad islands of Passamaquoddy Bay. Even Clamplain, the faithful chronicler, could keep no count of these islands. A vast sweeping curve of the shore, leagues in extent, clasped the sunny archipelago as a handful of jewels; and at the apex of the curve a broad river emptied itself quietly, between wooded low-lying lands, watched over by a solitary peak. This now they called the St. Croix, and on a little island within its mouth they resolved to set their colony. The waters round about were alive with fish, the islands in the bay with birds. At the south or seaward end of the island, which was long and narrow, containing about half a score of acres, rose a grassy knoll upon which to set their watch. Save for a stray elm or water-ash, the island bore but grass from brink to brink, and the two or three trees they found they cut down to go to the building of the fort. This was raised at the north end, and around it clustered the dwelling-houses, the storehouse, the chapel, and a great baking oven of burnt brick. On the main land near by they built a mill, and sowed, though it was now full summer, their rye and barley; and they laid out garden plots, in loving likeness to the thyme closes and beds of marjoren which sweetened the air around their Norman houses. Strange in their nostrils were the heavy aromatic odors of the wild parsnip, cloying the mid-day breeze. Strange in their ears was the intricate metallic bubblings from the bobolink's throat, the chide of the grackles in the alder and swaying elm-tops. They cut the elm for building and the alder for fagots, and the bobolink moved further off as he saw his loved wild-parsnip heads laid low. So with digging and building the summer passed merrily along. But, by and by, the summer went out in a sudden blaze of scarlet and gold; it

"Had glared against the noonday and was not;"

and a dispiriting greyness stole across the landscape. When the late October winds began to pipe over the shelterless island, bending the sere, long grasses all one way, and ridden by such a legion of dead leaves that every brook was choked and the still pools hidden from sight, their hearts turned homeward very longingly. At last the Acadian winter broke upon them, and it caught them unawares. The pleasant river grew dark, of the hue of steel, and chafed past their thresholds with a burden of ice and débris. The cold was such as France had never taught them to endure or to conceive of; sleet and pitiless winds drove in through the chinks of their rough walls, till they crouched over the meagre fires and grew sorely wretched at heart. No fuel nor water was on the island, and for both they had to face the fury of the weather and the danger of the sweeping ice-cakes. A band of Indians came to their camp upon the island; and the colonists, not yet acquainted with the friendliness and good faith of these "Iouriquois," were harassed with continual fear and watchings. Champlain's hope and cheerfulness nothing could daunt, and he strove to sustain the flagging spirits about him. But in vain. Then from their despondency and homesickness, from the cold on their bodies ill-inured to it, and from the salt unwholesomeness of their fare, came disease upon them. It was a plague, strange and terrible, for which they could find no remedy. The mouths of those stricken swelled, and their throats, till they were choking. Their teeth dropped out and their limbs, grown horribly enlarged, were altogether useless. So swift was the disease that hardly could the sick be given service, and the dead buried. When spring came, and kindlier skies, there remained alive but forty-four persons, out of a band of nearly four score; and these, as soon as strength returned, took ship with the first propitious weather. South as far as Cape Cod they searched the coasts, and found no place quite to their liking. But they had kept in mind the fertile valley and spacious sheltered basin of Port Royal; and thither they betook themselves, with whatever could be carried away from their sorrowful winter home. The fort and the walls of their dwellings they left standing, and they sowed the island with grain before forsaking it. The deserted walls soon fell, or were taken away by the Indians; and the stone and cedar foundations are buried under drift and river silt. The island has moved up stream a little, gnawed off to windward by the tides. But its shape is still unchanged, so that the ancient chronicle describes a familiar spot. The wind beats steadily across it still, the grass bending before it with desolate monotony; and save for the solitary light-keeper, who is there but from sunset to sunrise, the island is as empty of life to this day as when Champlain first dropped anchor in the St. Croix mouth.

FRENCH GARDENS, SABLE ISLAND.

"A land of sand, and ruin, and gold."

The question is almost literally correct. Scarce anything but ruin and sand, is the bane of ocean-farers, the "Isle of Sable." And though there may be indeed but little gold herein, yet there is no lack of costly merchandise washed upon its avaricious shores, and none can tell the riches that lie hid in "the sands" secretive bosom of Sable Island! It is a name to conjure with, raising, as it created, more phantoms than any other spot on the Atlantic. It is a name, when the fog is thick and the winds are veering fitfully off the south-east of Nova Scotia, to whiten the lips and cheeks of the hardiest mariner. The island has been given another name: "The charnel house of North America." Nevertheless, this place of horrors has a strange fascination for those who visit it, voluntarily! The sepulchre is well whitened. Though full of dead men's bones, the island is kind to its dead. The clean, unresting currents roll them and wash them, the clean sands swathe and cover them away. But one holds one's grave in this island on frail tenure, for the fickle winds and capricious waters love to uncover again even what they have most carefully laid from sight, and will shift one's last couch many times in the course of a quarter-century. After every violent gale, when calm has returned with clear nights, may be seen unknown bleached skeletons "revisiting the glimpses of the moon;" while others, by the self-same wanton gale, have been lapped away again in sandy burial.

The Isle of Sable is in great part a deposit of the drift of meeting currents. Vast eddies, from the contact of the gulf-stream's edge with two branches of separated polar current, circle about the island, eating away and rebuilding it continually. It is the nucleus of the densest fogs, the vortex of the wildest storms of the North Atlantic. Its shape is roughly that of a crescent, 22 miles long by one in width, and a shallow lake divides it longitudinally. It is moving eastward before the prevailing winds, and rapidly decreasing in size. When first set down on chart by Pedro Reinel, in 1505, its size was more than as great again as we have it now. On Reinel's chart its name is Santa Cruz. To a sheltered spot in the island, in honor of the earliest dwellers upon it, is given the name of the "French Gardens." The first settlers on the Isle of Sable became such by no free will of theirs; and this was the manner of their coming: In the Spring of 1598, the Marquis De la Roche, being made Vice-Roy of Canada and Acadia, set sail for his new dominions with a shipload of convicts for colonists. Approaching the Acadian coasts he conceived, in his prudence, the design of landing his dangerous charge upon the Isle of Sable, till he might go and prepare for them, on the main-land, a place of safety. As the French barque neared the island, and the eyes of those on board, though sharpened by weeks of sea-voyaging, could scarce distinguish, save by the settling fringes of white surf, the low grey shores from the gray tumult of surrounding sea, De la Roche felt that he might leave here his sorry settlers with a most reasonable confidence that they would await his return. The forty convicts, selected from the chief prisons of France, were landed thro' the uproar of the surf, and the ship made haste away from the perilous shore. But, she came not back again! De la Roche reached Acadia, chose a site for his settlement, and set out for the island to fetch his expectant colonists. But a great gale swept him back to France and drove him upon the Breton coast, where the Duke de Mercouer, at that time warring against the King, seized him, cast him into prison, and held him close for five years. Meanwhile, those left on the island were delighted enough. They were free, and began to forget the scourge and chain. Beside the unstable hummocks and hills of sand they found a shallow lake of sweet waters, the shores of which were clothed luxuriantly with long grass and lentils, and veins of vetch. Here and there were great patches of naked sand, and tracts where the sands had drifted over the grass and smothered it, but for the most part the valley of the lake was like a rolling meadow. No tree or shrub had root in all the island, but the turf where it was richest grew resplendent with wild lilies, and asters and dwarf roses. In some places the grass was thrust aside by the wiry branches of the blackberry, and whole acres were covered by a close mat of cranberry vines. Lurking in any or every portion of the grass-plain were little cup-like hollows, generally filled with clear water. These were formed by eddies of the wind, which kept scooping and sucking away the sand from every raw spot, where the skin-like covering of turf had been removed. The cups would then fill gradually from rains and from infiltration. Every such pool, like the lake, was alive with ducks and other water-fowl, amongst which the joyous ex-convicts created consternation. There were wild-cattle also, trooping and lowing among the sand-hills, or feeding belly-deep in the rank water-grasses; while herds of wild-hogs, introduced years before by the Portuguese, disputed the shallow pools with the mallard and teal. The weather for a while kept fine, and the winds comparatively temperate, and the sojourners held a carnival of liberty and indolence. But this was not for long, and as the skies grew harsher their plight grew harder. As the weeks slipped into months they grew first impatient, then solicitous, then despairing. Their provisions fell low and at last the truth was staring them in the face, they were deserted. From the wrecks upon the shore they built themselves at first a rude shelter, which the increasing cold and storms soon drove them to perfect with their most cunning skill. As their stores diminished they looked on greedily and glared at each other with jealous eyes. Soon quarrels broke out with but little provocation, and were settled by the knife with such fatal frequency that the members of the colony shrank apace. There was no discipline, no order, no authority. Every man made his own desire his law, and did his best to enforce it upon his neighbor. As they had been provided with no means of lighting fires, they soon had to live on the raw-flesh of the wild-cattle, and little by little they learned the lesson and began to relish such fare. Little by little, too, as their garments fell to pieces, they replaced them with skins of the seals that swarmed about the beach; and their hut they lined with hides from the cattle they had slaughtered.

The hut was built in the deepest heart of the island, in the firmest group of sand-hills they could find, for they had speedily learned to dread the winds that scourged that naked land with relentless fury. They built the walls about with turf and secured them with the heaviest timbers to be had. In the raving December nights, when the bitter cold edged through their thickest walls, they laid aside their feud and animosity and huddled together for the sake of warmth. Terror, too, drew them closer together, when the hurricane yelled about the sand-hills; when every one caught outside the hut had to throw himself on his face lest he should be whirled out to sea; when the darkness fell suddenly while they thought it scarce mid-day; when the only light was that from the driven spume; when the whole island quivered under the thunderous waters volleyed against it; and when the miles of beach were rent away to form new shoals in the offing. As the months became years their deadly contests ceased, but exposure, and frost, and hunger, and disease kept thinning their ranks. They occupied themselves in persuing the seal for its skin, the walrus for its ivory. The cattle they killed only to supply their needs; but the wild swine, grown bloodthirsty from having devoured dead bodies, they hunted down remorselesly as a hateful foe. And so the time dragged on, till they began to say they were nearly five years in this prison. They had gathered a great store of sealskins, ivory and hides, but now only twelve men remained to possess these riches. Their beards had grown to their waist, their skins were like the furs that covered them, their nails were like birds' claws, their eyes gleamed with a sort of shy ferocity through the long matted tangle of their hair. At last, from out of his prison, De la Roche got word to the King, telling him of their miserable fortune. A ship was at once sent out to rescue them, under the guidance of the pilot Chetodel who had sailed on the former voyage with De la Roche. They saw the ship at anchor outside the shoals and came down upon the beach, waving their arms. As they saw the ship urging to land thro' the breakers, they shouted and ran about like madmen, or cast themselves down grovelling in the sand, till their rescuers imagined them half-savage, half wild beast. Taken back to France with their furs and ivory, they were brought before Henry as they had been found, in their shaggy hair, and beards, and their coats of skins. The story of their grievous hardships moved the King, and he gave them money, with a full pardon; whereupon two or three of them went back to their island of horrors to collect more furs, and for the rest of their lives devoted themselves to that trade. The site of their hut, and of the sand-plot which they made an effort to till, has years ago been engulfed by the tides, and probably forms an outlying part of what is now called the Northwest bar. But the name, "French Gardens," keeps the story of their sufferings in remembrance; and the spot that bears the name is, by courtesy, the spot that gave them refuge.

THE ORDER OF THE GOOD TIMES.

As an offset to such a story of desolation, let me turn for a moment to the famous "Order of a Good Time." This institution, organized by Champlain at Port Royal, during the winter 1606-1607, has been well celebrated by the merry Max Lescarbot, a moving spirit in the Order. And it has been overlooked, I think, by no historian since. The temple of the Order was Poutrincourt's dark-ceilinged dining-hall, his ample dining-table the shrine of its most sacred mysteries. The initiated members were fifteen, and for guests, when they craved the spice of life, they had the great Micmac chieftain, with such of his warriors and wives as showed themselves most amenable to civilization. The office of honor and responsibility in the Order was the ancient office of steward, which fell to each member in turn, and was tenable fortunately, only a day at a time. Upon the shoulders of the steward there fell, with the decorated collar of his dignity, the burden of assuaging the appetites of this hungry and hilarious brotherhood. He had at his disposal no lack of stored provisions, bread, dried fruits, etc., brought from France by the previous summer's ship; but he would cover his office with disgrace if he failed to add some new delicacy to each new bill of fare. At first the task was not difficult, but as the various kinds of fish became familiar to the palates of the order, as another and yet another species of game was accepted and registered as satisfactory, the honorable steward was soon driven to tax his best wits. But there was never a failure, if we may trust Lescarbot's chronicle. Only, alas, toward spring, the wine ran low, and instead of three quarts to each member, the daily allowance was diminished to one poor pint. Canada's national beverage was not yet brewed, or they might have turned their rye to delightful account! When dinner was announced, the steward in his decorations led the way, bearing the staff and napkin of his office, and all followed in set order and solemn dignity, till the laden table was revealed in the glow of the heaped-up hearth, and the low-ceiling, with its shifting shadows, seemed to draw closer down about the cosy revel. The feast done, and grace said in grateful Latin, the steward rose and pledged his successor in a final magnanimous cup, and then resigned to him his badges and his burden. The effect of such an institution was to keep hearts and hands cheerful, and to speed the winter finely ; and though some of the colonists died before spring, Lescarbot sets this down to the fact that these were of a sluggish and fretful disposition and not susceptible to the curative powers of mirth. There is another and not unplausible explanation however, which Lescarbot strangely overlooks. Sometime during January the whole Order went on a six miles trip, to see if the corn they had sown in November was growing under the snow ; and there, in the snow and mocking sunshine, they held a picnic-banquet very gayly. This was a new and charming experience ; but the four deaths occurred not many weeks later! Poor sluggish, fretful souls!

THE WIFE OF CHARLES LA TOUR.

It is about this woman that chiefly clings the romance of Acadian history. Her is the name that stands in Acadian annals for heroism, fidelity, wifely devotion, ill-fate. Her's is a figure among illustrious women than which there is none bathed in a clearer and more stainless fame. Her's is the memory served with most chivalrous worship from the lips of us later Acadians.

On level land, well out of reach of high tides, on the inmost corner of that safe haven which lies at the mouth of the St. John, was built the fortressed home of Charles la Tour. It stood upon the harbor's western shore, over against a small island which ceases to be an island at low water, when the west channel, now called "Buttermilk Channel," for occult reasons has a trick of going dry. It was a strong fort of four bastions, heavily palisaded, and was the outlet for all the rich trade of the St. Johns River valley and eastern Maine. Within the fort were happiness and plenty, whether the master of the fort remained at home to rule as a kindly despot among his followers, or whether, during his long journeys into the wilderness, he left his wife to divide her time between her children and the government of the colony. The wife upon whose hands, with such confidence, he laid responsibilities so heavy, was a nobly-born and daintily-nurtured woman, who had left for him the luxury of a home in rich Rochelle. Love for their mistress, however, made the colonists easy to rule; and their time went by not idly, but with peace. There was trading with the Indians continually; there was the hunting and trapping; there were the long rows of stake-nets to be emptied of their salmon, and shad, and gaspereaux when the stony-flats east of the fort were daily uncovered by ebb-tide. So the days were filled up pleasantly at the mouth of the St. Johns. But across the fog and turbulence of the bay, in fair Port Royal, was creeping up a storm to mar this brightness. There sat the Sieur Charnisay, dividing with La Tour the Acadian territory and trade, and watching with vindictive envy the prosperity of his rival.

Already his enmity and diligent intrigues at Versailles were beginning to show their effects.

It was in the early spring of 1643, a dense, raw fog clung over the harbor and the heights. The tide was out; the flats stretched seaward their long lines of clean grey rock and their beds of olive kelp; the current of the great river swirled past sullenly with its sheets of whirling foam from the falls; the men, whose purple hands, numbed with the salt, were emptying the ranges of nets, loomed vague and distorted through the mist, and the voices of their comrades, whom the darkness hid, seemed wizard-like uttered from the waters. Suddenly the fog thinned, lifted, faded away into the blue of a sunlit morning; its last shreds streaming off reluctantly through the firs and cedars on the cliffs. The fish-gatherers, startled by an alarm-gun from the fort, looked up to find three vessels sailing in under what is now called Partridge Island. Following in the shadow of the same steep, dark-wooded shore, came several small crafts, pinnaces and cat-rigged launches. There was but little time left for taking counsel. All the colony was soon within walls, and the gunners stood to their pieces. Not bringing his ships within range of the fort's heavy metal, Charnisay choose a piece of smooth, red beach to the southward, where the waves lapped softly, and some cakes of ice still lingered in the shallows. Here he led ashore his five hundred men to the assault. By the half-dry channel to the left, by the dripping flats in front, by the naked uplands to the right, with shouts and volleys of musketry, the invaders stormed in. But La Tour was at home and not caught sleeping. For an hour the assault raged furiously on rampart and palisade and bastion, but the short carronades, with lowered muzzles, swept the ditches clear, and the besieged with musket stock and hand-spike beat down every foe that scaled the walls. Charnisay at last broke into an impotent rage, and ordered off his men to the ships; while the derisive garrison expediated their going with the acrid spur of bullets in their rear. Charnisay then drew a strict blockade about the fort and harbor, and waited for hunger to achieve what his arms could not.

But La Tour, like the Ithacan chieftain, was no less subtle than brave, and to hold him imprisoned was a feat Charnisay had not yet learned to perform. The Rochelle ship, long expected with supplies and reinforcements, at length appeared off the coast. Instructed by timely signals from the fort, she kept well out in the offing; and toward the close of a murky night a small boat slipped under her stern, and Charles La Tour and his wife were received on board. In shadow of the shores of the harbor and Partridge Island heights, favored by the first of the ebb and a gentle wind off shore, with muffled oars they had crept through the blockade, and were off for help to Boston ere the dawn. The help was got, and all haste made back to the rescue. As Charnisay rested on his decks, dreaming that his foe was pinched with famine, his triumph now surely close at hand, as a most unpleasant revalation came La Tour with five ships and bore down upon him ready for battle. But he had small stomach for the encounter, and standing not upon the order of his going, the whole force took flight for refuge in Port Royal. As he reached Port Royal, La Tour was on his heels chastising him upon his own threshold. The quarrel might well have been ended then and there, to the sparing of much misery in the future, but the scruples of his Puritan allies, who were fairly well content with the booty already fallen to their hands—a cargo of rich furs belonging to Charnisay—here stepped in and proclaimed the virtues of moderation.

These half-measures, as La Tour well knew, could profit his cause but little. Charnisay was not enfeebled by this repulse; fortified, rather, in his purpose, strengthened with a more inexorable will of revenge. In silence both antagonists braced to renew the struggle. La Tour set himself to repair his defences, while his wife undertook a voyage to France to gather men and supplies and to strengthen the hearts of her husband's friends in his cause. To France also had gone her enemy before her, to plot and scheme at court, to borrow money, and to heap up false accusations against La Tour. After the manner of a mean nature toward whatever most shames it by contrast, Charnisay appeared to hate the wife even more bitterly than the husband, and no sooner learned of her coming than he brought a charge of treason against her, and obtained the King's order for her arrest. But the lady had been watching his every move, and now, as more than once thereafter, over-matched him. She made a seasonable departure for England, and from London organized her husband's relief. By the spring of 1644, she had a vessel chartered and set sail; but the captain consumed the whole summer in trading by the way. It was September when she reached Acadian waters, where Charnisay was on the watch for her, and straightway boarded the ship. She and all her party were hidden in the hold and the ship was represented as a trading-vessel bound for

Boston blown far out of her course by adverse winds. Beguiled by this possible story Charnisay retired; the vessel's course was mended for Boston, and the brave wife landed on Boston wharves just too late to see her husband sail away. He, filled with fear at her strange delay, had once more come to Boston for assistance; but this time on a futile errand, for the Puritans would hazard in his cause naught more costly than their sympathy and good wishes, and he had gone away at last with plenty of smiles upon his lips but with something near despair at his heart. But his wife, her hands now free, lost no more time. Bringing action for the unwarrantable delays she was adjudged two thousand pounds damages, in satisfaction of which she immediately seized the ship's cargo. Meanwhile arrived in the city an ambassador from Port Royal, seeking peace between Charnisay and New England. Hearing of the lady's presence the envoy made great haste with his business, and having persuaded the non-committal Puritans into something like a treaty he departed from the city the same night. His hope was to give warning at Port Royal in time to capture this dangerous adversary before she could get behind the walls. But the servant succeeded no better than his master had done before him. As he came before Charnisay with his tidings, the brave wife was in the arms of her husband from whom she had been parted during thirteen months of fear. This was in October; and Charnisay now for a time sat quiet with his wrath, which required little nursing to keep warm. Not till the following February did he judge his vengeance ripened to the plucking. His needs had driven La Tour again to Boston. On the news of his going came the grim craft of his enemy, appearing swiftly in silence like a shark, and took station under the lee of Partridge Island. The winter days wound by on tedious feet, under leaden skies for the most part, and through rainy winds and sleet. But on sharp blue mornings the watchers on the ramparts could see flitting whitely across the furthest tides, the cruisers of Charnisay waiting to intercept the longed-for relief. Within the fort, in spite of the wearying suspense, the garrison maintained good heart, scorning to be any less heroic than the dauntless woman at their head. As venison, fish and flour got low, the monotonous strain on their spirits grew more intense, till even attack would have been hailed as a fortunate change. Then came the excitement of finding traitors in their midst, and two friars, spies in conspiracy with Charnisay, were uncloaked with fierce curses and contempt. The garrison was for hanging them forthwith from the battlements, but their leader's too compassionate heart forbade it. She contented herself with driving them from the fort, from whose gates they slunk, white with terror and tremulous with malice, like lashed hounds to their master. Their words were exquisite to the ears of Charnisay. They told him of a feeble and dispirited garrison; of little powder, and that hurt by the wet; and of his long-craved triumph now within the very grasp of his fingers. The gray spectre of a ship that had so long lurked in the shadow of the dark island, was now seen to glide from her moorings. She drew silently up the harbor, lay to under the walls, then burst out against the fort with the roar of all her guns. But the sullen walls, so long seemingly dead, from which he had expected scarce a retort, awoke straightway to most retaliatory life. Every bastion blazed, and Charnisay's spars flew in splinters under the storm. The garrison went wild with the delight of battle, as their beautiful leader—for she *was* beautiful—encouraged them, and moved where peril was the thickest. She went from bastion to bastion, and would take no shelter that covered not her followers as well; her clear eyes seemed everywhere at once, marking with grateful approval the brave loyalty of the least of her men. As her form from time to time appeared to those on shipboard, through the dividing drifts of smoke, the lips of Charnisay set themselves with yet more implacable hatred. The clear stretches of snow at the rear of the fort, the dazzling capes upon shoulders of fir-tree and cedar on the uplands, turned swarthy-brown as the smoke-waves volumed over them; and the tide-eaten ice-fringe was blackened along the shore under the battle. Soon the concentrated fire from the ramparts began to tell heavily upon the vessel's hull, her rigging being already a mass of wreck. When a score of men lay dead upon her decks and everywhere lay the wounded, Charnisay would still acknowledge no repulse. But when it was found that the hold was filling rapidly, with deep curses he turned for flight while flight was possible. But it was barely possible. Ignominiously beaten by a woman, whom he had attacked when he thought her nearly helpless, he got out his small boats and hawsers and painfully towed his sinking hull out of range. He ran her ashore for repairs upon a strip of sandy beach; and as soon as she could be kept afloat and steered he put back to Port Royal, balked once more. But he had the whole of France open behind him, while the adversary under whose chastisement he now writhed was so utterly shut off from all resources that the very nights and days fought against her. Her victory even seemed to presage defeat. Her enemy, when he again attacked, would more justly have measured her strength. Her husband could neither break nor elude the fast blockade which Charnisay's deadly vigilance maintained. And through the lull that followed their success it seemed to the waiting handful in the fort that the end of their grim play drew swiftly near.

With the first of April weather, the climax came. One still night, when the sentry could hear the far-off rush of the falls, could hear the weird honking of the wild-geese, streaming northward unseen through the starless night, his ears grew suddenly alert as he caught also a distant rattle of cables, voices of sailors, and the splash of lowering boats. The fort was astir at once; lights glimmered here and there and were afterward extinguished and all made ready for the struggle that was expected with the dawn. With the dawn it came. The foe had disembarked in the night, and now made the attack upon the landward and weaker side. Fiercely the stormers advanced to be doggedly and defiantly hurled back; but with the defenders it was an energy that hoped for nothing. They, as well as their leader, knew that now finally had fate declared against them. From Thursday until Saturday the unflinching woman fronted every charge, and against her indomitable courage the enemy broke and fled away shattered. Charnisay paused for a breathing spell and the garrison rested heavily. At length a stranger in the fort, an alien coward, turned traitor and, with the enemy's gold warming his pockets, admitted them when it came his turn on guard. Even then, though to the garrison all was lost, Charnisay was not yet victorious. Within walls he was met so desperately that a mean fear seized him lest again he should suffer the shame of defeat. He felt the pre-eminence of the woman who faced him, and inwardly quailed before her. He called out for a truce, and offered honorable terms. Seeing that the day was surely his, however this agonized resistance might be dragged on, and longing with her whole heart for the safety of her people, she set her name to the articles of surrender. Then came the supreme hour of the dastard victor's baseness. Even at this day as one tells it a fierce heat pricks in one's veins. When his end was gained, the stronghold in his power, his great rival crushed under his heel, then Charnisay mocked the woman he had so hardly vanquished, and tore up the capitulation before her face. The heroic garrison he took man by man, and hanged them in the open yard of the fort, while their mistress, sinking with horror, was held to watch them with a halter about her neck. The hideous deed finished Charnisay took his captive to Port Royal, where he presented her to his wife with mock reverence, as his deadly foe taken in by him to be cherished. But his taunts or his malignance to her were nothing; she had no heart left for any further pang. Within three weeks from the ruin of her husband, the destruction of her home, the butchery of the loved and loyal followers, the wife of Charles La Tour died, with bitterest foes and strangers watching her.

AN ACADIAN "BUCHE DE NOËL."

At this season it is appropriate that I should close with some faint echoes from an old Acadian Christmas.

It is December 25th, 1610 Anno Domini, and the tiny colony at Port Royal is five years old. The sun has risen just clear of a range of encircling hills, white with new snow. The whiteness is cut sharply here and there by sturdy fir-trees that have shaken the snow from their overladen boughs and now tower erect in the sparkling air, while their feebler fellows bend to earth under the weight of their snowy capes. Were we nearer we should find these unimprisoned trees girt about with a tangle of rabbit tracks and the dainty foot-prints of squirrels, the snow beneath the branches spotted with half-gnawed fragments of fir-cones. The level sunshine streams down the valley to the little palisaded fort at whose gate we are standing; it dazzles over miles of white plain, then out upon the bosom of the land-locked harbor of Port Royal. In the distance and out of our ken, beats the tide-chafed mother of fogs, the Bay of Fundy. The blue and golden surface of the harbor is flecked with ice cakes from the Port Royal river, which is soughing in its channel close beside us. The tide is out, and the stream's bed is choked with ice-cakes, huddled thick together; but along high water-mark the ice is laid in order, like mighty armor-plates of crystal, soiled at the edges and weather-eaten. The sobbing in mid-channel, the low noises of grinding and crumbling, and the signs of the incoming tide, lifting the ice. At the head of yonder little island the floes have shouldered one over another above tide-level, and with their clear facets have built up a mighty cluster of prisms. The snow that has wrapped up everything, climbing the palisades of the fort, hiding the ditch, curving over the low eaves of our poor half-dozen cabins, is trodden well down before the door of the forge and strewn with great fragrant yellow chips. The forge fire is out to-day, black as the store of charcoal heaped behind the anvil, and firewood in liberal lengths is piled up higher than the eaves. As we mark each detail in this our live spot in the expanse of gleaming desolation, and note how the smoke from fort and cabin curls dusky orange against the hard blue sky, a restless-looking, dark-faced man, in deerskin tunic and creased voluminous boots comes out of the fort and plies the axe with vigor upon a huge trunk of dry pine. At the sound of the axe-strokes an Indian cur appears stealthily, and sits down in front of the chopper to observe his work. As the chips fly thick and fast the dog moves to a safer distance. Then a cabin door opens, and the inviting roar of a fire streams out into the frost. The chopper hesitates, leaves the log unsevered, enters and shuts the door behind him; while, stealthily as it came, glides away the Indian cur.

This is the quiet of Christmas morning at Port Royal, two hundred and seventy-six years ago. No clamoring of bells, no laughing shrill voices, no idly hurried crowds as in their own dear Picardie and Normandie. Jean de Biencourt, Baron Poutrincourt, has with him twenty-three persons in this little lonely colony. No need of work or haste this Christmas morning; and their work is, for this day at least, done. They have drawn in the yule log, with abundance of cut firewood; and though they have by no means too much venison in store, they have worn themselves out in the hunt and need not take it up again till the morrow. So they idle about, and

―――"Dream of fatherland,
Of child and wife,"―――

till it shall be time to gather in the chief room of the fort and eat their poor Christmas dinner. They are depending almost wholly now upon such fish as they can catch through the ice, and on the game they capture for themselves or buy from the friendly Micmacs near at hand. Their grain, corn, barley and a little wheat is all but gone; the longed-for vessel from France still delays; and it is doutful if they can succeed in staving off absolute famine. But for this one day at least, they will not stint themselves, though moose-meat and fish become sorely monotonous to their palates.

The night before they had lighted the yule log with brave cheerfulness and good fellowship, had welcomed the feast with firing of guns, and had initiated the convert Memberton with his braves, into the blessed mysteries of the season. Father Flèshe had summoned them in toward midnight, and mass had been celebrated with single-hearted fervor indeed; but ah! with what a difference from the services even then, as they knew, being offered up in lighted aisles and chancels far away. They had thought of the sea of upturned faces, rapt and moveless, as the shepherd-priests came forward reverently and the curtain was drawn back to show the Virgin and the Child. Again in their ears rang the soaring flawless treble of the hidden boy, singing as an angel, the *Gloria in Excelsis*. Again, as they chanted with closed eyes, they heard the full responses, the clanging of swung censors; they saw the ranks of surpliced priests and singers bow together; and the aromatic breath of incense stole into their nostrils. But it was only a handful of exiled and weary men, singing at midnight in a rude half-lighted room; outside their walls the limitless Acadian wilderness, and a thousand miles of wild seas between themselves and home. Then, for some, as they turned to their blankets, what aching of heart to see no little shoes set out in prime order before the fire-place, expectant of toys and sweetmeats from *Jésus Bambin!* And for all of them, the coming festival could be but a season of longing and of looking back. This was their Christmas eve!

To-day, as the hours wear on, the stories they have been telling come to an end; the pine-trunk by the forge-door has been more than once attacked spasmodically, till it bears no remotest resemblance to its former self; and the savors of venison and fish, and of hot cakes of broken wheat, attract attention. The fire in the chief room blazes higher and higher. Snow-shoes hang on the walls, or stand in the corners in a confusion of muskets, and hand-nets and long ashen paddles. Over the windows are moose-hides tanned with the hair on, heavy black bear-skins, and furs of lynx and *loup-cervier*, out of which, as a faint gust stirs them, gleam polished claws and white snarling teeth. The warriors invited to the feast squat at one side on their deer-skins, and the sober revel begins. The courses are few and little varied, but the dinner is by no means one of herbs. Yet is it a feast where love is, and the red guests pledge to their entertainers unending fealty; a pledge destined never to be broken. Then follows stories, and encounters of wit, and remembrances, and toasts; speeches are made, prophetic of a new and mighty nation to spring from the heroic effort of their own small band; and *A la Claire Fontaine* is sung, with other loved old songs. As night falls, a wind roars in from the sea, full of drift and of the sounds of crashing ice, and lashes wildly roof and palisade. Some paddles and snow-shoes fall to the floor with loud clatter. Then the fire on the wide hearth blazes up redder than ever, hissing and sparkling fitfully; the company draw closer to the blaze, shutting off the light from the further draughty corners; dark faces glow and moist eyes gleam as they watch the flame intently, fallen into silence; and our picture fades out into the dimness of three centuries ago.

In conclusion, a brief glance at the modern Acadian Christmas! In Madawaska County, New Brunswick, leagues inland from the beating of sea-winds, or fertile banks of the St. John and Green River, the Madawaska, Quisibio, and other lovely streams, the Acadian now builds snugly his wide-eaved cottage, setting an orchard about it, amid fields of flax and buckwheat, and painting his broad barn-doors and the vane of his inevitable windmill of the crudest ochreish red. At Christmas the snow has fallen all around him to the depth of five or six feet, his fences and boundaries are obliterated, his roofs scarce rise above the encompassing levels. Indoors the fire lights up his shelves of blue and white crockery. There is no chilly plaster to be seen. The ceiling is of wood darkened with years and smoke. The one partition, dividing his abode into living-room and sleeping-room, is of wood, polished by the rubbing of hands and shoulders. The massive square bed; the square cradle that rocks with dreadful thud, loud enough to keep a baby wakeful a whole life-time; the square table; the spinning-wheel that could not well be square — all are of the same brown, solid, shining wood. On Christmas eve there are the guns and shooting, the drive in the pung, half filled with quilts and straw, to meet at the little chapel miles away; and on Christmas day the fiddle reigns supreme. Neighbors flock in, and moccassined feet dance indefatigably, morn and noon and night. Huge slices of sweet bread, such has been made for this feast out of plain dough kneaded up with molasses and spotted with dried blue-berries, and washed down with a wholesome beer made from spruce boughs and juniper berries. Sometimes the "national beverage" plays a modest part. Not seldom, as it grows late, the dancing palls, and the singing. Then, as of old, all gather round the fire; and if, as often happens, a modern cooking-stove has supplanted the open hearth, they provide themselves with large raw potatoes, from which, with their clasp-knives, they shave thin slices artistically. The next point is important; they spit on these slices, and then fry them to a turn on the hot black covers; and the sizzling and aroma fill the air. If the hearth still holds sway, each arms himself with a slim green sapling, whereon he toasts red herrings for the damsel of his heart, who sits beside him. The children of the house, meanwhile, from under parti-colored coverlets, stare through the open doorway with unwinking eyes, too early exiled from the circle, but solaced with peppermints and delicacies which the Good Angel, acquainted with the corner grocery, has brought them in their sleep the night before. So the day, and the night, draw to a close. And if the mood of the party has been a merry one, the cocks, perchance, are crowing under the snow-muffled sheds, the last stars fading out on the biting, grey-blue sky of dawn, as the guests race away in a confusion of jangling bells, and straw, and snorting of the ponies.

173

COMMERCIAL UNION BETWEEN CANADA AND THE UNITED STATES.

BY
Hon. B. BUTTERWORTH, M. C.

Read before the Canadian Club of New York.

Y heartiest thanks first for the honor of addressing you this evening.

It is my purpose to discuss the merits of full and complete reciprocity of trade and commerce—commercial union, if you please—between the United States and the Dominion of Canada.

Import and export duties are levied fort two purposes.

First—To collect revenue to defray the expenses and to pay the debts of the government.

Second—To encourage, foster, and protect domestic industry.

The protective system, as it is called, has for its object to do away with the inequalities which obtain between competitors in this country and those of the old world who are engaged in the same industrial fields.

Protection was not intended as an agency for the mere increase of profits; consequently the question which should be considered by Congress is not simply that of the magnitude of profits resulting from manufactures established under its wings, but the question is whether we should be able, without the protective duty levied on articles of commerce produced in the old world, to engage successfully in manufactures at all. The question is whether the perfected plans of the older countries, the rare skill of its workmen, resulting from the accumulated experience of years, together with the abundance of cheap labor, does not enable European manufacturers to lay down goods at our doors cheaper than we could possibly produce them; and whether money invested in a shop, mill or factory, in view of such competition, is not an absolute loss.

This does not apply with so much force to the agriculturist who can compete with the world in the growth of agricultural products. The protective tariff naturally raises the price of all the articles upon which a duty is imposed, and the cost of most of the articles the farmer uses, except those he produces himself, is thereby enhanced. The farmer found a compensation under the protective system in the fact that, under the development of our industries, great cities and towns grew up, and markets for the products of the farms were thereby created. What the farmer lost through the increased cost of the articles he purchased, he more than made up through the increased amount he received for the supplies he was enabled to sell to those employed in the industries which owed their existence to the protective system. But, as a tub to the agricultural whale, a tariff was levied also upon farm produce.

The European manufacturer and merchant cannot dispose of a plow, a trace-chain, a knife or a hoe upon our market without paying a large tax to our government for the privilege. Nor can the foreign merchant sell us a yard of cloth or silk, or a quinine pill, until he has paid the duty levied by Congress. Of course this is all paid at last by the consumer, who finds a compensation for the alleged burden in the prosperity of his country, brought about in the manner I have mentioned. The tariff is a law arbitrarily enacted by Congress—there is but one party to its formation. It is a system with which the nation resorting to it has alone to do.

It should and does ostensibly deal with unequal conditions in the field of competition, its mission should be that of equalizing them. It follows logically, and as a common-sense proposition, that when the conditions are equal, so-called protection is disguised robbery, legalized filching from one citizen to enrich another citizen.

Reciprocity of trade involves an agreement between two nations, according to the terms of which, trade and commerce are to be carried on between the people of the two contracting nations.

The proposition in the instance which concerns us, the merits of which I shall discuss, is that of a full and complete reciprocal trade and commerce between the United States and Canada. By its terms, for all purposes of trade, barter and exchange, the two countries shall be as one country. There being no necessary connection or relation between the political institutions of a country and its trade and commerce, the arrangement has nothing to do with government matters or political conditions. By this arrangement we seek to remove all the custom-houses along our Canadian frontier, to withdraw the line of pickets that keep watch and ward on both sides along 3,000 miles of our northern boundary, in order that, on the one hand, the American farmer shall not sell to his neighbor across the line some early potatoes or early corn without first going to the custom-house and paying a large part of the value of the produce for the privilege; while compelling, on the other hand, the Canadian to submit to the same extortion before he can sell to his friend who supplied him with the early corn and potatoes a later variety of the same articles. We propose—as the inhabitants of what should be considered, for all trade purposes, a common country, being in race, religion, ancestry and tradition one people, and differing only in our political institutions—to throw down the barriers that now block every highway of business prosperity and progress, and open all the courses and channels of trade between the Gulf of Mexico and the northern boundary of the Dominion of Canada. We propose that the farmer, the manufacturer and the merchant shall, unhampered and unrestricted, seek markets in every part of this vast field of development, and thereby settle at once, and in a manner worthy of our race and civilization, the petty squabbles about the fisheries now more than a century old. He who appeals to the protective system between competitors in Canada and in the United States, asks for monopoly not equality. He seeks an unjust advantage, not an equal opportunity.

Both Americans and Canadians may invoke the protective system against the whole world, but the system has no proper place between Canadians and Americans, unless authorized extortion in the interest of monopolists should be the proper aim of legislative effort.

There is not a condition, there is not a worthy interest involved in the proposition that does not cry out against the present system and in favor of the fullest reciprocal trade.

Careful investigation will disclose that the growth of our industries is in a large measure the result of our system of patent laws, which has funded and multiplied industries almost beyond computation. It is well to understand which are the actual sources of our prosperity. I have not time to discuss at length this factor of the problem; therefore I shall proceed with the main question, the nature of which I have endeavored to explain.

The adoption of the proposed system would involve an assimilation of tariff rates and internal revenue taxes, and possibly an arrangement for pooling receipts from customs, and a division on some equitable basis—all of which, as it has been fully demonstrated, present no serious difficulty or embarrassing problem.

The details of the arrangement I do not propose now to discuss. It is enough to remark that once the policy being decided upon, its execution will be an easy matter.

The times and the conditions into which both countries are placed force this question upon public attention.

It is said that unsettled public questions have no pity for the repose of nations. The truth of that saying is fitly illustrated by the disturbing influence of the unsettled fisheries question between the United States and Canada. It stands, and it has remained since the treaty of Paris, a constant and threatening menace to the peace and repose of both nations. It has been a barrier to trade and commerce between the two countries. It relates to but a single industry, and efforts have been repeatedly made to settle it without reference to interests with which, in the future of things, it is inseparably intertwined. The question is not a new one, nor does it now for the first time force itself forward and challenge the thoughtful consideration of both nations. It relates to the rights and obligations of the fishermen of the two countries to catch fish in certain localities and to sell it in certain markets. Relating solely to the privileges of a few thousand fishermen engaged in a single avocation, it draws into the vortex of the controversy, nevertheless, all other trade and commercial interests between the two nations. Canada and the United States are contiguous. They both formed a part of the Dominion of Great Britain. The colonists of the United States of to-day bore their share of the burdens and endured hardships and fought to establish the sovereignty of the British flag in what now constitutes the Dominion of Canada. The history of the Dominion, so far as her political relation to the mother country is concerned, is much the same as that of the United States. In that respect, the experience of Canada is about the same as ours; the only difference being that England, under the influence of a riper and more enlightened civilization, inspired by broader statesmanship, in which the sword played a less conspicuous part than formerly—accorded to Canada prompt redress for her grievances, recognizing the necessities of the situation and the inexorable logic of the time. The careful student of history will discover that the demands of the Canadian provinces, upon the mother country, for larger powers and wider jurisdiction in the management of their affairs, were of a nature and extent which outstripped the original demands of the American colonists. While entertaining and cherishing respect and affection for the mother country, Canada, in the school of experience, learned of her needs; and, in a manner which suggests something more than firmness, petitioned for relief which was granted sooner or later. The restrictions and the burdens imposed upon the trade, commerce and the manufactures of the colonies by the mother country were intolerable. No people fit to be free, and being at all worthy of their English ancestry, could submit to them. However, Canadians did not submit. Whether themselves and the world in general have been the gainers on that account, future events will show.

It is exceedingly interesting to note how like suppliants the colonists approached the mother country and sued for relief against laws confessedly oppressive and whose administration was intolerable. Observe the manner in which our cousins on the North stood and demanded what experience had taught them proper as belonging to a free and enlightened people in the matter of self-government. Long ago, England decided that free-trade was best for her interests; but not until she became, under a different system, the workshop of the world and mistress of the seas.

So far as the colonists themselves were concerned, her restrictions upon the trade of her American colonies had little of the flavor of free-trade about them.

Virginia was required to ship her tobacco to England in English vessels solely. England interposed her authority to paralyze every manufacturing industry in the country. Such a condition of things could not last, and we were finally compelled to set up for ourselves, but not until we had helped to establish the sovereignty of the British flag over the country north of us. In 1763 England sent to Canada her first Governor-General. In the latter part of the eighteenth century the legislative bodies of Canada had but little power; but during the last fifty years the Provinces were not slow to demand such enlargement of the powers of their home governments as were required by the people. England acceded, though not always with good grace, to the point that the destiny of Canada, by common consent, is to-day practically confided to Canadians. If Canada's past belongs to England, her future is her own. The growth of the country in substantial independence and through the management of her own affairs has in no wise disturbed her filial regard for the mother country. When I say the mother country, I mean the people of England, not the English government. I make this distinction because there is a broad difference between an affectionate regard for the people of a nation and an unquestionable loyalty to the governmental policy which that nation may see fit to adopt. I was devotedly attached to my father: I loved and honored him. I might not have felt great enthusiasm for his disciplinary ideas about household matters after I had acquired a home and a family of my own. Canadians have the best of reasons to cherish the deepest and sincerest affection for their English ancestors. But neither involve the surrender of independence of character and action which are inseparable from worthy manhood, a quality which is bound to assert itself, not only in those things that concern the individual, but also in affairs of the State.

I am addressing Canadians whose loyalty cannot be doubted. If I refer to the history of the course pursued by the United States and Canada towards the mother country, it is only to show that what has been sought in the past as well as in the future is the freedom, prosperity and happiness of the citizens of each nation; in fact they have been treading the same paths in order to attain a similar end. Canada remains loyal to England because the latter has granted her those rights and privileges, a denial of which to the colonists of the Republic drove them into emulating the example of their English ancestors, namely, suing for them or fighting for them if need be.

The controversy about the fisheries is a quarrel between ourselves. It is for us to settle and to adjust that controversy in consonance with enlightened principles and a fair regard for the rights, duties, obligations and interests of both nations. Hitherto a settlement has been impossible because negotiations were carried on from the English stand-point of the economic principle which should govern trade and commerce between the directly interested parties. Under such circumstances, a permanent and lasting solution of the question was tantamount to impossibility, and had to remain so as long as English interests, as contradistinguished from those of Canada, were to be first considered. No full and final adjustment can ever be reached on the matter, except through negotiations between those immediately interested and who are to be affected by them, and these are the provinces of Canada and the United States. The adjustment must not be based upon the idea or theory that the fishing interests are to be segregated and treated as if they stood apart and alone, free and disassociated from other interests, industries and avocations. Any settlement that should have for basis anything in view except that of securing the greatest good to the greatest number, would be partial and unjust, and would be a false premise.

The fisheries imbroglio had its growth in the following manner: Prior to the American Revolution the inhabitants of the English dependencies in America enjoyed in common the fishing grounds in the neighborhood of Nova Scotia, Newfoundland, and in the bays and gulfs in those localities. The treaty of 1783, at the termination of the war of the Revolution, defined in a vague manner the rights and privileges of the people of the United States to the fisheries. Innumerable controversies were constantly growing out of alleged trespasses by one or the other party, and armed cruisers were kept in those waters to protect the rights of either parties.

The treaty of Ghent, which was signed at the end of the war of 1814 (December, 1814), is silent on the subject of the fisheries. Subsequently, England showed a disposition to treat the omission as a surrender by the United States of their positive rights to the fishing privileges theretofore enjoyed by Americans. England's interpretation of the omission was not allowed by the United States, so the dispute went on and threatened, from time to time, to culminate in war. In 1851 the relations of the two countries were strained to the last degree, I mean the relations between England and the United States—Canada was merely considered then as the cause of the quarrel rather than a party to it. In fact, Canada was the little boy whose big brother had borrowed the quarrel. Observing statesmen on this continent viewed the question in its true and logical aspect, and the United States and Canada maintained that the controversy involved something beyond the interest of the respective parties in the fisheries. In their estimation the question embraced the trade and commerce between Canada and the United States, and they maintained that the only possible and lasting adjustment was one which would place the trade between the two countries on a reciprocal footing. But this could only be effected by a treaty with England. Such favor did reciprocity of trade find in this country that in 1848 the House of Representatives passed a bill enacting its establishment. John Quincy Adams was a member of that House; so were Robert C. Winthrop and Abraham Lincoln. The attitude of the Whigs toward reciprocity may be inferred from the fact that the party had a majority of ten in the House which passed this bill, whilst the Senate was Democratic. However, the bill failed to become a law because it came too late before the adjournment of the

Senate, for that body to give it proper consideration. This happened under the administration of Fillmore, of which Daniel Webster was Secretary of State, and Wm. H. Seward Senator for the State of New York.

In closing his speech on the subject of the fisheries, Mr. Seward said :

"What the colonies require is some modification of commercial relations which may affect the revenue. That is a subject proper to be acted upon by Congress. Let us no longer excite ourselves and agitate the country with unavailing debates, but let us address ourselves to the relief of the fishermen and the improvement of our commerce. There is only one way that Congress can act, and that is by reciprocal legislation with the British Parliament or the British colonies."

And he further asks whether some reciprocal legislation cannot be adopted to adjust these difficulties and at the same time consistently enlarge the rights of our fishermen with the various other interests of the United States.

The wisdom of those who adopted that view has been attested by time and experience. Partial reciprocity came in 1854, and only failed in its mission because it was partial, unequal, and in a measure unjust. It is believed that Canada had the advantage in that arrangement. However, the treaty which secured a partial reciprocity proved the adequacy of the remedy if fully and properly applied.

In 1874 President Grant, in furtherance of this policy, negotiated a treaty establishing in part substantially what is now proposed. The treaty, which was negotiated by President Grant and Secretary Fish on the one hand, and Sir Edward

Thornton and the Hon. George Brown, Commissioners for the Provinces and Great Britain on the other hand, contained the following propositions, I quote from a report semi-officially submitted by Mr. Brown to the Canadian Senate:

"The draft treaty embraces ten propositions: 1. The concession to the United States of our fisheries for twenty-one years, and the abandonment of the Washington treaty arbitration. 2. The admission into both countries, duty free, of certain natural products therein named. 3. The admission, duty free, of certain manufactured articles therein named. 4. The enlargement of our Welland and St. Lawrence canals. 5. The construction of the Caughnawaga and Whitehall canals. 6. The free navigation of the great inland lakes and of the St. Lawrence River. 7. The concession to each other, on equal terms, of the use of the Canadian, New York and Michigan canals. 8. The reciprocal admission of vessels built in one of the countries to all the advantages of registry in the other. 9. The formation of a joint commission to secure the efficient lighting of the great inland waters common to both countries. 10. The formation of a joint commission to promote the protection and propagation of fish on the great inland waters common to both countries."

The proposed Caughnawaga canal was intended to connect the St. Lawrence river at Montreal with the northern end of Lake Champlain. The Whitehall canal was intended to connect the Hudson river at Troy with Lake Champlain at Whitehall.

By referring to the list of articles covered by this treaty, it will be seen that it is free from one of the objections contained in the reciprocity treaty of 1854, as it was proposed to admit into the Canadian markets the products of our factories, which were excluded by the treaty of 1854. The list covered by the treaty is as follows: Agricultural implements, of all kinds; axles, of all kinds; boots and shoes, of leather; boot and shoemaking machines; buffalo robes, dressed and trimmed; cotton grain bags; cotton denims; coton jeans, unbleached; cotton drillings, unbleached; cotton plaids; cotton ticking; cottonacks, unbleached; cabinet ware or furniture, or parts thereof; carriages, carts, wagons and other wheeled vehicles or sleighs, or parts thereof; fire-engines, or parts thereof; felt covering for boilers; gutta-percha belting and tubing; iron—bar, hoop, pig, puddled, rod, sheet or scrap; iron nails, spikes, bolts, tacks, braids, or springs, iron-castings; India-rubber belting and tubing; locomotives for railways, or parts thereof; lead, sheet or pig; leather, sole or upper; leather, harness or saddlery; mill or factory or steamboat fixed engines and machines, or parts thereof; manufactures of marble, stone, slate, or granite; manufactures of wood solely, or of wood nailed, bound, hinged, or locked with metal materials; mangles, washing machines, wringing machines, drying machines, or parts thereof; printing paper for newspapers; paper-making machines, or parts thereof; printing type, presses and folders, paper cutters, ruling machines, page-numbering machines, and stereotyping and electrotyping apparatus, or parts thereof; refrigerators, or parts thereof; railroad cars, carriages and trucks, or parts thereof; satinets of wool and cotton; steam-engines, or parts thereof; steel, wrought or cast, and steel-plates and rails; tin tubes and piping; tweeds, of wool solely; water-wheel machines and apparatus, or parts thereof.

It will be observed that the proposed treaty embraced those articles which are in daily use among the people, and such as are needed in leading industries. It aimed specially to help those branches of industry in which the citizens of both countries were alike engaged in, and to exempt those articles in which considerable traffic was likely to take place.

While commenting upon the merit of this treaty, a leading statesman of Canada, the Hon. George Brown, and as already stated one of the Commissioners for Great Britain, said:

"The first, second and seventh propositions go naturally together, and they need no comment. They embrace simply the conditions of the old treaty of 1854, which operated so favorably for us, and so much more favorably for the United States. I will leave it for the present and return to it again.

"The fourth proposition—for the enlargement of our existing canals—is one eminently for the advantage of the United States, and involves a very large expenditure on our part. It is impossible to estimate the enormous annual gains that must result to the farmers of the Western States, when vessels of 1,000 and 1,200 tons shall be able to load in the upper lake ports and sail direct to Liverpool—free from transhipment expenses, brokers' commissions, way-harbor dues, and ocean port-charges, and return direct to the prairies with hardy emigrants and cargoes of European merchandise. Canada, no doubt, would have her share of benefit from all this—but it could not be compared for a moment with that of the great Northwestern and some of the Middle States.

"The fifth proposition—for the construction of the Caughnawaga canal—would be also an immense boon to the United

States. It would open up to the dense manufacturing population of New England, for the first time, a direct water communication of their own with the great West; it would enable them to load ships of 1,000 tons at their Lake Champlain ports with merchandise for the prairie States, and bring them back freighted with farm produce; and when the Whitehall canal should be enlarged to Troy, and the improvements of the upper Hudson completed to deep water, where in the wide world could be found so grand a system of internal water navigations that, stretching as it then would, in one continuous ship channel from New York on the Atlantic to the west end of Lake Superior, possibly ere long to the eastern base of the Rocky Mountains. Canada, too, would have her share of profit in all this. Her great lumber interests on the Ottawa and its branches would find full advantage from it, and the enterprising farmers of the midland and eastern counties of Ontario would have the New England market, with its three and a half millions of manufacturing population, open to their traffic.

"The sixth proposition is the concession to each other of the inland coasting-trade, and nothing could be done more sensible or more profitable to both parties. Our season of navigation on the lakes is short the pressure for vessels in particular trades at special times is very great on both sides of the lakes, and freights advance to unreasonable rates. Cheap transportation is a foremost question in this Western industrial world, and what can be conceived more absurd than to see, as is often seen, large quantities of produce lying unshipped for want of vessels, because foreign bottoms cannot take freight from one port to another in the same country? What the

United States could fear from the competition of our limited marine with the 5,576 vessels of all kinds and an aggregate tonnage of 788,000 tons, it is difficult to imagine.

"The eighth proposition—for the reciprocal admission of vessels built in either country to registry in the other—is generally regarded as highly advantageous to this country, and no doubt such is the fact. But I confess I cannot see why it ought not to be regarded as infinitely more advantageous to the United States. During the civil war the merchant vessels of the Republic were sold in large numbers to foreign owners, and acquired foreign registers, and notwithstanding that shipbuilding had almost disappeared from the United States in consequence of an extreme protectionist policy, the law absolutely forbade their being brought back or vessels of foreign build being purchased in their stead. The consequence is that, at this moment, nearly the entire passenger traffic of the Atlantic is in the hands of foreigners—a vast portion of the freight of merchandise from and to foreign countries is also in the hands of foreigners—and only two months ago we had the startling statement made officially by Mr. Bristow, the very able Secretary of the United States Treasury, that no less a sum than $100,000,000 is paid annually by the people of the United States to foreign ship-owners for freights and fares. Now, a large portion of these ships, which the people of the United States require so urgently, can be as well built in St. John and Halifax and Quebec, and at less cost than in any other country. Why, then, deprive the American citizens of the privilege of buying them from us and sailing them as their own? We are told that American shipbuilding is reviving;

but were it to revive with all the rapidity the most sanguine could desire, it could not keep pace with the wear and tear of the present reduced marine and the annually increasing demands, much less begin to supply the *vacuum* created since the war.

"The ninth and tenth proposals are for the appointment of joint commissions for the care of the light-houses and the fisheries of the inland waters common to both countries; but as to these there is no difference of opinion, and no doubt of the great mutual advantage that might flow from the proposed concerted action in regard to them."

This treaty did not fail by reason of its not finding favor with the Senate. It was laid before that body only on the 17th of June, 1874, and so near adjournment that there was not time for its consideration.

The propositions show how broad and sweeping the contemplated changes would have been. Had the treaty been consummated it would have been one of the most brilliant achievements of President Grant's administration, as it would have removed the last barrier which intercepts the natural and healthful flow of trade between Canada and the United States. In course of time, the advantages of such reciprocal relations would have become so manifest that not a vestige of our system of custom-houses and tolls—system which has nothing to commend it—would have remained to tell of the strained relations which had formerly existed between England and the United States.

During the last days of the Forty-ninth Congress, I introduced a bill which provided for securing full, complete and unrestricted trade and commerce between the sixty millions of people of the United States and the five millions of Canadians, who are not only our kinsmen, but our nearest neighbors— in fact, to all intents and purposes, of our very household. Though somewhat crude, the bill clearly shows the way to attain the object in view.

It is suggested that there is some doubt as to how this proposition would be received by the American people. First, let me tell you that it is not a party question, and that it has been received with general favor by the leading journals of the land. It is a proposition above the level of mere partisan expediency, and it appeals to a higher motive and nobler ambition. It is a question of public policy affecting the people of both sections, and will be so considered by our people. It involves, of course, a revision of our tariff, and this may suggest a party aspect; on that score it may be opposed by those who are reaping large benefits from industry which are specially and extravagantly protected. However, it does not involve the abandonment of either free-trade or protective theories. Whether it is made a party question or not, the party lines cannot be drawn closely when the question is presented for action. There are times in the United States—even when party feeling runs high—when the whippers-in, detailed for the service, are incapable of either muzzling their partisans or absolutely control their votes. I have every reason to believe that the policy adopted by our government in the matter of establishing reciprocity with Canada will appeal to the independence of our law-makers, and that caucuses, which have especial reference to mere party advantage, will not be allowed to control adversely the action of Congress.

In discussing this question we have to bear in mind the relative physical conditions of the two countries. The territory of Canada is interlocked with our own. The rivers and lakes which are our common highways of traffic and trade cross the boundary lines. Canadian public highways are also ours. Therefore, the relation of our territory to that of Canada, the location of our rivers, the natural facilities of both for conducting exchanges, all suggest and plead for unhampered reciprocal trade. The resources of Canada in material wealth, her supply of the materials indispensable to our people, are boundless. On the other hand, we have an exhaustless supply of those things which are prominently indispensable to the comfort and enjoyment of our Canadian neighbors. Hence the advantages to be derived from free commercial intercourse. We are not dealing with a people across the ocean, but with our neighbors and kinsmen.

It is not my purpose to read statistics. Statistics are dry, and unless studied with care they are apt to mislead. If figures do not lie they may be made to prevaricate most abominably. It is chiefly with the philosophy of the situation I purpose to deal to-night.

It is from the stand-point of dollars and cents that I propose to study the situation. First, let me ask you who are the parties to the controversy? with whose interests are we dealing?

If we leave out of the question the matter of revenue for the support of the government, I insist that unless it be the mission of both governments to sacrifice the interests of the many for enriching the few, the present system which compels our Canadian neighbors to pay a high duty on fifty millions of dollars worth of goods a year for the privilege of supplying to the citizens of the United States articles indispensable to their comfort and prosperity, and which on the other hand compels the citizens of the United States to pay a like sum into the public treasury of Canada for the privilege of doing like service for Canadians living across an imaginary line, I say the system is absolutely defenceless, inexcusable. It is not sufficient to show, even if it was a fact, that certain industries prosper under such a system. It must be shown that the system promotes the general good. In other words, to be equitable, the prosperity resulting from any governmental system must give equal opportunities to every citizen. The system if at all defensible, is solely so on account of needed revenue.

To illustrate the character of the trade between the United States and Canada, I have procured a statement of the imports from Canada and the exports to the Dominion since the year 1850 to 1878 inclusive, covering the period of partial reciprocity inaugurated in 1854, and which ended in 1866. Of her products, Canada sold to the United States in round numbers, during that period, $700,000,000 worth—lumber or timber heading the list. During the same period we exported to Canada $848,000,000 worth of our goods. I should be glad to learn how either Canadian or Yankee prospered by reason of the immense tax levied upon the goods so exported or imported. I should be glad to learn of the blessings derived through paying for duties one-third of the value of the goods so exchanged? How our people were benefitted? Those who used these goods in this country or Canada, paid for them a price largely in excess of their value, because they were produced on one or the other side of an imaginary line which marks the frontier between the United States and Canada. Certainly that in this instance protection is inapplicable and detrimental.

I am a protectionist. We are largely indebted to that system for the marvelous development of our industrial arts. One article in my political confession of faith favors the protection of infant industries, so that they may acquire sufficient strength to enable them to stand independently in the field of competition. But that article of faith, mark you, only refers to infant industries, and not to full-grown industries capable of maintaining themselves against all competitors. To protect industries without reference to condition is to create monopolies, the over-weening influence of which would be more dangerous to liberty than the crown of a queen.

My countrymen would deserve contempt if they sought protection against Canadian competition, and—with all due respect for the worthy gentlemen who met at Toronto to speak about the manufactures of Canada—I have as little consideration for the Canadians who pretend that their countrymen are lacking the ability, the enterprise, the resources necessary to hold their own against the United States in any field of industrial effort. In my judgment, protection between the United States and Canada means no more and no less than the taking of money from the pocket of one citizen and of putting it into the pocket of another, the latter belonging to the protected and favored class.

As stated in my opening remarks, protection, as I understand it, relates to and deals with unequal conditions, and has no other just mission than to equalize those conditions. It is not intended to harden the lot of the many in order that the few should rejoice in prosperity. To protect one class of citizens against another class, in any field of effort where the conditions are identical, is wholly defenceless. In my opinion, nothing is easier than to defend the protective system of the United States against competition from the old world. It would certainly be difficult to explain a similar system between the Eastern and Western or the Northern and Southern sections of the United States, and such a system is equally indefensible when applied between Canada and the United States.

I refer to this matter at this time because my position on the question of a commercial union is in perfect harmony with my convictions upon the subject of protection, inasmuch as I am a protectionist of a somewhat ultra school. I contend, and the matter is too clear to need argumentation, that there is as little reason, abstractedly, to restrict or in any wise hamper the trade between the United States and Canada as there would be in imposing similar restrictions and burthens upon trade between the inhabitants of Ohio and those of Illinois and Iowa. I have already stated that a protective tariff must have for its sole object the equalization of abnormal conditions. If it be true that prosperity comes simply through a protective tariff, without reference to general conditions, and that we become rich and prosperous by levying duties upon all we buy, provided it is produced elsewhere, while being fenced by the same operation out of every market to which we should sell, then why should not each State in this Union become speedily rich and prosperous by simply erecting a tariff fence as between itself and the other States of the Union? It is true the Constitution forbids this, but I am discussing the abstract proposition. As a measure, if it is justifiable in the case of Canada, because it insures prosperity to its people adopting it, why is it not equally admissible between the various States? They might become prosperous by adopting that system against sister States, and since prosperity is one of the high-roads to happiness, have we not found out the royal road to prosperity and happiness by taxing ourselves and recognizing the right of our neighbors to tax us also? What has been heretofore considered a burden, would become at once a help and support! The principle applied to Quebec and Ontario and the other Provinces would make them speedily prosperous. It is what Mr. Wiman described as the process of taxing one's self rich.

Unless it can be shown that there is something in the situation and condition of Canada which makes the case exceptional, and takes it out of the comparison I have drawn, the system we have pursued against our neighbors, and they against us, is as indefensible as it would be for Pennsylvania to seek the prosperity of all her people by a protective tariff against Illinois—Illinois being more largely an agricultural State than Pennsylvania; or, to put the case more strongly, as indefensible as it would be for Illinois to establish a tariff for the benefit of her citizens against Connecticut and Massachusetts, the latter being manufacturing States while the former is largely agricultural. Careful students are aware that the laws of compensation are immutable. Trade and commerce seek natural channels: manufactures ultimately will, other things being equal, locate nearest the base of raw supplies, otherwise it would involve the shipping of material a thousand miles to be first manufactured and then the reshipment of the finished product over the same line to find a market.

In so far as the citizens of the United States are concerned, what are the objections to commercial union? I hear and know of none except some of a local character. It may not be amiss here to call attention to the fact that one of the leading statesmen of the day, one who has filled possibly a larger place in the public mind than almost any other man of our day—I allude to James G. Blaine—has advocated, and most ably, a commercial union between the United States and the South American States. His proposition met with general favor, and was not considered as a mere party question. If great advantages are to be derived from a commercial union with South American States, how much greater and important are the advantages to be gained from intimate trade relations with those upon our immediate border and to whom we are allied by ties stronger than those which relate merely to commerce, and with whom our trade, although they number but five millions, is larger than that of the forty-five millions lying south of us and with whom a commercial union is proposed. I will submit a statement which indicates how much more valuable Canada is to the United States as a market than all the realms lying south of the Rio Grande, including Mexico and the South American States.

During the year 1885 the United States sold to all the Central and South American States but $27,000,000 in round numbers, and to all countries south of the Rio Grande, an aggregate of $64,000,000. To the 45,000,000 of people in the south we sold $64,000,000, while to the 5,000,000 of Canadians we sold over $50,000,000.

If our hampered and restricted trade with 5,000,000 Canadians now reaches over $50,000,000, what will be its extent when the blockade is removed, and when our neighbors shall number 25,000,000 of people?

Do American manufacturers fear competition? Certainly not. Do American manufacturers and merchants desire the Canadian market with its great possibilities? Certainly they do. Does the American farmer fear the competition of the Canadian farmer? The proposition is simply absurd. No possible conflict of interest on those scores. On the contrary, experience abundantly proves that unrestricted and direct exchange between the sources of supply in either country would give a new impetus to every branch of trade and industry and result in a great era of prosperity to both nations. In this connection it may be well to note that we are accustomed to explain to the agriculturist, and to all those interested in the tilling of the soil, that their prosperity has been brought around by the protective system which made markets for their grain and other products. In a great measure this is indisputable. But if we examine the statistics which furnish us with the range of prices for farm products during the last sixty years, we find that, whatever may have happened to other branches of industry the prices for farm products have not substantially advanced.

To prove the correctness of my assertion I will read to you a list of the prices which obtained at various times during a period of sixty years.

I quote New York prices and take them from the Trade Reports: For instance, in 1825 the price of flour in New York ranged from $3.50 to $4.25 a barrel. At the close of the following five years, that is in 1830, from $4.75 to $6 a barrel. In 1835, from $5.37 to $7.87; and in 1840, from $4.62 to $6.50; and in 1845, from $4.31 to $7; in 1850, from $4.93 to $6.25; in 1860, from $4.25 to $5.25; in 1870, from $4.50 to $6.05; in 1880, from $3.75 to $5.75; in 1885, from $2.90 to $3.70, and in 1886, from $2.65 to $3.50.

If we turn our attention to the article of fish, with its flavor of actuality, we find that the price of mackerel in 1825 was from $5 to $5.75 per barrel. In 1835, it was from $6 to $8.25; in 1845, from $11.50 to $14; in 1855, from $18 to $22; in 1865, from $15 to $25; in 1875, from $7 to $24; in 1885, from $14 to $24; and in 1886, from $15 to $29. Compared to the farming industry, it is difficult to see how the fishing industry has suffered. The range of prices has been decidedly in favor of the fisherman.

Let us consider the article of beef, mess beef. The range of prices by the barrel has been about the same. In 1825, from $8 to $10; in 1835, from $8 to $13.50. In 1845 it was lower—from $5.50 to $9.75; in 1855, from $8.25 to $14; in 1865, which was during the war, it ranged from $9 to $14; in 1875, from $8 to $10; in 1885, from $10 to $16; and in 1886, from $5 to $12. The range of price in hams has varied but little.

Corn has ranged about the same for the last sixty years.

All these figures relate to the New York market. The opening of the great commercial channels—railroads and canals—has resulted in equalizing prices, so that to-day it is no longer profitable to burn corn in the great West.

In wheat the range of prices has not been any more favorable to the farmer. The price ranging from 75 cents $1.06 in 1825; from 83 to 95½ cents in 1886.

Mess pork ranged from $12 to $14.75 in 1825; from $9 to $14.50 in 1885, and $10 to $12.50 in 1886.

In the meantime, farmers and producers generally have had to face a large increase in the rates of wages. True, on the other hand, that the facilities for farming have also greatly increased, so much so that to-day one man can double or triple the task that he could accomplish formerly; thus reducing to a minimum the apparent increase in wages.

It must not be forgotten that certain climateric conditions affecting the farmer may come to pass which no system or legislation can control—the rain and the sunshine—his crop depends upon the earlier or the latter rains. Nor can any system of law regulate the yield of land in case of a drouth or a superabundance of rain; not so with the manufacturer, because the products of the factory can be controlled, the output limited and the prices determined. The competitors of the American farmer for the European market are not to be found in Canada, but in India and Russia. During the past year Canada produced only about seven per cent. of the wheat grown on the North American continent.

The change will affect undoubtedly some special interests; but I do not believe that the fishing interest will be seriously crippled ; nor can I concede that the fishing fleet which supplies the army or the militia of the sea will suffer from a fair competition between the Canadians and the New England fishermen. If, under such conditions and with fair competition, we cannot hold our own on sea and land, the fault must be attributed to conditions which are not to be righted by the levy of a tax increasing the price of every codfish-ball and every mackerel which is placed upon our table.

So far as the timber interest is concerned it has no proper place in our system of protection, the object of which is to build up industries. But, unfortunately for the timber industry of this country, the more it is protected, the more it is cherished, the more speedily it dies, and we are and have been taxing ourselves upon every shingle we use and every beam that we require to construct a dwelling, not to make strong an industry that will flourish and grow, and furnish a more ample yield, but simply to pay a bonus to certain individuals who have prospered beyond measure, and without any corresponding benefit to the great mass of the people of this country upon whom the tribute is levied.

The Canadian forests are almost limitless. Their timber is rotting and going to waste, while the citizens of the United States are paying enormous prices for a supply to construct houses and make shingles to cover their heads, and thousands of mechanics are idle for want of the material—lumber—to enable them to prosecute their calling. Idle men on both sides of the line is the direct and necessary result of our absurd system. It is not only absurd, but an outrage upon our people, when one or two industries are permitted, nay, authorized for their own benefit, to tax every other vocation, trade and calling in this country, and thus impose needless burthens. The time has come when both burdens and blessings should be more equitably distributed, and what is proposed here is a step in that very direction.

Now, with your indulgence, I will consider for a moment the objections raised by our friends across the line to the consummation of full and complete reciprocity. First, they object to it by saying that such a system would be destructive to the manufacturing interests of Canada. Second, that it would be treason against the mother country; that it is, in fact, the essence of disloyalty, and that its ultimate result would be annexation to and absorption by the United States. Lastly, it is urged that the mercantile interests of Canada would suffer, and that drummers from New York and Boston would absolutely destroy the trade of Montreal, Quebec, Toronto, Hamilton and the other leading cities of the Dominion; that the revenues of Canada would be lost.

I notice, Mr. Chairman, that a leading journal of Toronto remarks that you and I were born twenty-five years too late for all purposes of reciprocity and commercial union between Canada and the United States; and in the same article it is suggested that a quarter of a century ago this matter might have been favorably considered, but now it cannot be. Attention is called in this connection to the fact that there must be borne in mind " the expenditure of the past twenty years in railroad construction, in acquiring territory, and in various ways having in view inter-provincial trade and the development of Canadian national sentiment through closer inter-provincial commercia relations, the purpose being to do away with unnatural barriers, and allow each Province to cultivate the trade adjacent to it." The argument submitted by the learned editor defeats itself. The only purpose of improving the railroad system of either country, and of improving the water-ways, is to enable the producers to reach the markets of the world. If they serve any other proper purpose it is difficult to understand what it is.

It is also suggested, as a part of the criticism of the policy of reciprocity, that the system and efforts before referred to—improved agencies for commercial intercourse—were made to do away with the unnatural barriers between the Provinces and to cultivate the trade adjacent to them. This is pertinent, and suggests that all barriers that block the natural highways of trade and commerce should be removed. It suggests also that it is natural and proper to cultivate trade which is near at hand rather than seek distant markets, especially when better ones lay at our very doors. This is precisely the object for which patriots on both sides of the line, in Canada and the United States, are struggling.

The point made in the same article, that drummers from New York and Boston would destroy the mercantile business of Canada, is hardly worth considering. The argument has been met and answered a hundred times, and the experience of every-day life absolutely shows how fallacious it is. If the objections mentioned were well taken, it must follow that there would not be a healthful mercantile business carried on in any of the cities of the great West. Certainly New York and Boston would have no advantages over Canadian cities that they do not have over the towns and cities of the great West. To pretend that the rival competition of New York and Boston would destoy the mercantile interests of Canada is tantamount to asserting that the merchants of Canada and Canadian enterprise belong to a former century, and to a people who do not possess the aggressive energy and merit to compete with all comers in an even field of business venture.

It will be remembered, in this connection, that there was at one time, among men representing important eastern interests, much opposition to the enlargement of the facilities for transportation along the line of our northern frontier, whether by our Canadian friends or our own people ; it being urged that it would open up a line of travel, a commercial highway if you please, which would cripple the middle and southern lines of trade and commerce. Time has demonstrated the absolute falsity of this pretension Men have only to rightly consider the elements entering into the solution of these various problems to discover that the law of compensation operates everywhere.

It is urged by certain honorable gentlemen in Canada, and by some in this country, as an objection to the measure, that the move in the direction of commercial union seeks ultimately, and has, in fact, for its prime object, the annexation of Canada to the United States. Do gentlemen believe that annexation would follow commercial union? If so, upon what do they base their conclusion? Does Canadian prosperity involve annexation to the United States? Does Canadian prosperity involve disloyalty to the British crown? If so, why? Is there anything in the relations of Canada to the mother country which suggests that prosperity can only come to Canadians by severing their connection with the English government? It would seem that gentlemen who insist that prosperity means annexation must conclude that annexation is indispensable to Canadian prosperity and happiness. I do not agree with them. Canadians are satisfied with their form of government, and there is no desire on this side to change it, nor yet to have them adopt any one phase of our own. We can work out our destinies side by side. That in many respects, we must and will have one common destiny, I have no doubt. We are one people to all intents and purposes, so far as Christian civilization and the end it seeks is concerned; and, so far as the things to be attained by the growth and extension of that civilization require a common purpose and a common effort, we will, whatever the respective forms of government under which we live, be one people. Commercial union is in no wise inseparable from annexation. One does not involve the other, unless the fact that such a union banishes all possibility of attrition between the two countries and puts the seal to a bond of perpetual peace between them, can be construed as evidence of a desire for annexation.

I may here call the attention of the honorable members of this Club to a few facts bearing upon the history of Canada and her relations to Great Britain. I have already alluded to it. Gentlemen, of course, are aware that the tie which binds us to Canada has little to do with commerce—nor do I speak now of political relations proper, but of those relations that grow out of kinship, similar language and similar religion—all of which have little relationship to commercial intercourse. If Canada finds no closer tie between her people and those from whom they are descended than that which is born of trade and commerce, it is a matter of little consequence how soon those ties are severed. The history of Canada and of the United States, so far as England is concerned, is identical. The record of the history of Canada during the last half century discloses the fact that her complaints against the mother country have been similar in character to those which compelled the American colonies to petition for redress of grievances. Canada complained of the navigation laws so far as they were applied to her. Those laws were modified or absolutely changed. She insisted that it was her right to have her internal policy regulated by representatives chosen by the people who were to be affected by that policy. That privilege was also conceded. She demanded, furthermore, the right to collect and disburse her revenue according to her own ideas of internal economy. That also was conceded her. She asked, in effect, that she should be sovereign, within her borders, upon all matters pertaining to the civil administration. That too was conceded, and these just concessions—barring the mere matter of kinship, the ties of common ancestry, of a common religion if you please, and of those ties which naturally grow from similar institutions, and, as I believe, from a common destiny—have above all else preserved to this day, among Canadians, the spirit of perfect loyalty toward Great Britain.

The fear that Canada will be absorbed by the United States, or that she will lose her independence and dignity as a sovereign nation, is absurd in itself. Whether she shall stand among the nations of the earth, great, rich and independent, will depend upon the character of her people and the manner in which she utilizes her vast resources. Her mineral wealth invites the most desirable immigration. Her vast forests are only awaiting for hardy pioneers of enterprising spirits to pursue the various avocations dependent upon a supply of timber The same is true of her other resources.

I observe also that it is asserted by some writers in the Canadian press that an arrangement, such as the one contemplated, would be in the nature of an alliance offensive and defensive with the United States as against Great Britain. This is so far from being the case that the assertion must be regarded as an appeal to prejudices rather than an appeal to the intelligent judgment of our Canadian friends.

It is not for the mere advantage which is to be computed by dollars and cents that, as an American citizen, I urge full reciprocity with Canada. It is to secure, not a bond of political union, but a bond which will keep the English-speaking race one people now and for all times to come, and enable it to fulfill its mission by developing the highest and best form of civilization the world has ever known.

The resolution adopted by the gentlemen who met in Toronto, asserts: "That unrestricted reciprocity in manufactured goods would be a serious blow at the commercial integrity of the Dominion, and would result disastrously to their manufacturing and farming industries and other financial and commercial interests." The farmers, at least, had spoken for themselves, and their resolution was certainly the outgrowth of intelligent investigation and a just appreciation of what was essential to create prosperous conditions. I doubt whether the honorable gentlemen who adopted that resolution represent the sentiments of a very large portion of those among the people of Canada who, in the last resort, are to bear the burthens of what is dubbed the N. P., in other words the National Policy of Protection.

Did it ever occur to our manufacturing friends in Toronto that the resources at their command, which are almost illimitable, must attract in their midst that activity and energy which, after all, makes a country great and prosperous? That such would be the final result all history abundantly attests. Possibly, Mr. Chairman, if reciprocity had obtained twenty-five years ago, we would not have been honored by your presence and masterly entreprise in New York. In fact, this Club might not have been in existence. The energy which you have put forth here would have found such profitable employment on the other side of the line that you would not have come among us; but your friendship for us, and ours for you, would not have been a whit lessened by the fact of the prosperity which waited upon each country.

Whatever may be said to the contrary, I take it from the discussions in the English Parliament that England will not feel greatly disturbed over a commercial union between Canada and the United States. Able discussions in that body, as to the effect of protective tariffs, indicate that it is the opinion of English statesmen that whatever advantage may accrue to the protected country, if any, no disavantage will result to England. Such is the statement made by Mr. Chamberlain, and his statement is supported by figures, cited in his speech of August 12, 1881, in reply to an Address from the throne which urged retaliatory measures against nations exacting high duties on goods imported from England. I have here the speech of Mr. Chamberlain, and have been interested in observing how thoroughly his conclusions are sustained by the statistics he cites. I regret that I have not time to read portions of it.

I think careful investigation will demonstrate that industries which in Canada should need protection against European competition would, in the United States, require an equal protection ; and that a protective system which in its operation would be of benefit to Canada would be equally beneficial to the United States, and *vice versa*. Duties would, of course, in a large proportion, be levied according to the amount of revenue necessary, the protection in a large mesure would be merely incidental.

It is suggested by certain gentlemen, and I speak of this because I am addressing Canadians, that the proper thing would be a reciprocal arrangement between England and Canada through which the former should discriminate against the farm produce of other countries. This would be a very remarkable proceeding indeed, as it would add to the price of food on every laborer's table in England in order to obtain a market for the output of British factories. Outside of the indefensibility of such a scheme, it is unlikely that England would consent to tax the bread and potatoes and the meat of her workmen merely to attain the possible advantage of a new market in which to sell the products of her shops.

So far as the agricultural interests of this country and Canada are concerned, it must be conceded that they are not susceptible to secure a hearing with the same ease as the manufacturers, the merchants and financiers who are more immediately connected with trade and commerce. The cities are centres of political influence, and also centres of trade and financial power; therefore, those interests, that are the competitors of agriculture, not only have more ready access to the public ear, but they have moreover the sympathies of those who command the most ready means for controlling the current of public thought.

I would call the attention of the speakers at the late manufacturers' convention at Toronto, and the editors who echo the sentiments that have been expressed there, that the prosperity they would secure to Canada by defeating any attempt at reciprocity, unless it be one-sided, would be a prosperity of such a character that it could not be shared in generally by the mass of the people on either side of the line.

The time has come when the burthens and blessings incident to national development and healthful growth must, as nearly as possible, be shared equally by all; and I think we may rejoice in the fact that the farmers, artisans and producers in Canada and the United States will no longer, without rebuke, permit those who alone profit by a protective system which does not deal with and correct unequal conditions, to assume to represent and speak for all who have a right to be heard upon the subject.

It is impossible to see how any Canadian or American interest could suffer by the establishment of an active and healthful trade between the two nations. It is equally difficult to see how a growing tide, swelling every artery of commerce, reaching from every part of Canada to the markets of the United States, and from every part of the producing sections of the United States to Canada, and meeting the demands of the people, could injure any business interest fit to survive. To my mind at least, such an assertion is absurd, and I greatly doubt if it has its origin in a patriotic love of country. There is about it a savor, if not a positive suggestion, of selfish interest.

I note what is said touching the destructive influence that free international commerce would have upon the fisheries and some other industries. It is asserted with great force, and seemingly the assertion is sustained by statistics, that free fisheries mean the absolute destruction of American fishing interests.

In reply, I have to state that if the American fisherman, when placed upon equal terms, is unable to compete with the fisherman of Canada, it does not prove the former's inferiority in any respect, nor his inability to accomplish what the Canadian, under similar circumstances, can accomplish. It only proves that there is something wrong in our policy or in some part of our governmental machinery; it proves that oppression in that business drives from its arena Yankee competition hopeless and crushed, and that the remedy must be sought in some other direction, as it assuredly cannot be found in driving such competition from our midst by oppressive legislation.

If we are unable to hold our own in the field of open, free and equal competition, we had better improve our stock. I am for America and American institutions and interests, first, last and all the time, but that point is not at stake here. The question is how shall we build up every American interest worth cherishing, and how shall we avoid to build up one interest at the expense of the other, since we are aware that otherwise our industrial growth would be neither healthful or permanent?

If any industry in the United States cannot survive the competition of our immediate neighbors, only divided from them as we are by an imaginary line, the cause for such failure on our part must be sought in some unwise feature of our governmental policy, and not in the superior merit of our competitors in that industry or enterprise. Unless I am in this respect convicted of error, I am unwilling to admit inequality on our part with any nation in the world competing with us under circumstances substantially the same, and I would be ashamed of the Canadian who would not make a similar assertion concerning his countrymen.

I have already commented upon the proposition which pretends that it is the mission of the government to provide such artificial conditions that it shall be as profitable to cultivate the impoverished soil of New England as it is that of the rich valleys of the Mohawk, or of the Scioto and the Wabash.

In that respect I have only to say that the moment the government will make such an attempt, I will earnestly favor revolution. In this country we are not wanting in soil sufficiently rich to feed the world, and those sections which are not fit for profitable cultivation can be either abandoned, enriched by private enterprise, or used for other purposes than farming.

Our transportation facilities are sufficient to feed those

localities where the manufacturing industries are located. The law of compensation applies. If New England finds farming unprofitable, she can find profitable employment in various kinds of manufacturing. Her people, if not producers of corn and wheat, are nevertheless producers of plows, hoes, trace-chains, and thousands of other necessary articles. The genius of her sons has brought them riches, in fact, they are the bankers of the United States, and eastern thrift has been so great that the capitalists of that section hold mortgages on a large percentage of the farms in the West. I trust that if the time has not yet come, that it is not far distant, when the government will be engaged in some other mission than that of multiplying blessings for the few through an inequitable distribution of the public burthens.

This question should be considered by every board of trade, every chamber of commerce, every agricultural association, every society composed of manufacturers and producers generally.

Congress has and will have no official judgment upon it. The boards and associations I have mentioned must do the legislating—Congress is only a sounding-board, a cave of echoes, an assemblage of unpatented graphophones, repeating what is talked into them by the people.

Congress is engaged for the most part in formulating into law the popular will, and by no means do I think the term "popular will" to be synonymous with intelligent public judgment. As individuals, Congressmen have intelligent convictions; they are capable, conscientious men; but it is not their province to attempt to form or direct the public mind. Their mission is to respond to the public will. A Congressman's duty is to agree with his constituents — this is the essence of his political life — and it is not at all likely that he will consciously commit political suicide.

It naturally follows that you are to determine for yourselves and the country whether the immense volume of our trade shall be dammed up and rolled back upon ourselves, and whether a system which smacks of a primitive period and a ruder and less advanced civilization, shall continue to dwarf our enterprise and retard our development.

216

*Then came men with eager eyes,
And talked of steamers on the cliff-bound lakes;
And iron tracks across the prairie lands;
And mills to crush the quartz of wealthy hills.* —CRAWFORD

THE MINERAL RESOURCES OF CANADA.

BY
JOHN McDOUGALL.

Read before the Canadian Club of New York.

HOSE who are familiar with this subject know its vastness, and how impossible it will be to do it justice in the limited time at our disposal. We can only skim over it, and the references made to it will necessarily be imperfect. We can only give a passing glance at some of the principal minerals, and to present them in such a way as will impress you with the fact that Canada has the possession of untold wealth in them, and only waiting for the means for their development.

The Laurentian range of rocks on the Atlantic coast, and running inland through the Provinces of New Brunswick, Quebec and Ontario, are of the oldest known formation, and they contain almost all the known minerals. On the Pacific coast and throughout British Columbia and a portion of the Northwest Territories, the rocks are similar to those of Nevada and Colorado. That immense territory presents to capitalists and miners a field for their enterprise, acknowledged to be, without any exception, the finest in the world; and no country is endowed with such magnificent waterways; these, in addition to our canals, and over 12,000 miles of railways, give easy access to nearly every part of the country, from the Atlantic to the Pacific. Mining in Canada has been carried on only to a limited extent thus far; lately, however, a great interest has been made manifest by the formation of new companies with large capital. We are satisfied, from what we know of existing companies, to predict good dividends for all investments made for the development of mines.

I will touch on different minerals in alphabetical order, and will begin by drawing your attention first to—

APATITE.

Apatite is known in commerce as "Phosphates." It is generally of a greenish color and of a crystaline formation, and is found in great abundance in the Provinces of Ontario and Quebec. Apatite is used for the mannfacture of phosphoric acid and phosphorus, and enters largely into the composition of certain porcelains. It is, besides, very extensively used as a fertilizer of the soil. Phosphates are among the minerals most essential to vegetation, and are removed from the earth in large quantities by growing crops. To render it fit for agricultural purposes, it is converted into a soluble salt, which is known as superphosphate of lime.

The apatites of Canada are the purest met with, analysis of cargoes running as high as 37 to 39 per cent. of phosphoric acid, equivalent to from 80 to 86 per cent. phosphate of lime; the percentage shown is higher than that of any other country. The mines in the valley of the Ottawa River have become famous, and are extensively worked. This industry ranks now as a most important and profitable one. The output for the year 1885 was about 24,000 tons.

ASBESTOS.

Asbestos is the commercial name of a variety of the hornblende family of minerals, of which the chemical composition is chiefly silica, magnesia, alumina and ferrous oxide. It is a fibrous mineral, noted for its power to resist fire and acids.

Other uses to which it is put are fire-proof cements and putty, for joints, and in the manufacture of fire and acid-proof lumps, blocks and bricks. The ordinary gas fire is familiar to every one, and it will suffice to point out that asbestos enters largely into the composition of the artificial fuel upon which the success of the fire in a great measure depends. This mineral presents a very wide field for the inventive genius to open up a new process to dress it, so that it can be woven into fabrics of every kind as easily as with cotton and wool, as well as for many other purposes for which it might be made suitable. It is largely mined in the eastern townships of the Province of Quebec.

ANTIMONY.

Antimony is mined in the Province of New Brunswick. The Surveyor-General of that Province reported some years ago, that the mining companies there should be able to produce antimony at such a low rate, and in such quantities, as would place the Province among the great antimony-producing countries of the wold. Its analysis varies from 61 to 69 per cent. It occurs also in the Province of Quebec, Megantic County, both in the native state and as sulphurate.

BARYTES.

Barytes, or heavy spar of fine quality, is found in very great abundance in the Provinces of Ontario, Quebec and Nova Scotia. Very litlle has been done yet in mining this material except in Nova Scotia.

BITUMINOUS SHALES.

Extensive works were operated in Nova Scotia for the manufacture of oils from shale, but had to be abandoned in consequence of the heavy import duties imposed by the United States. The yield was about 60 gallons of oil from 1 ton; they were also capable of yielding 7,500 cubic feet of gas per ton.

COAL.

The coal area of Canada is very extensive—an approximate estimate places it at 97,000 square miles. The Provinces of Nova Scotia, New Brunswick, and British Columbia, and the Northwest Territories, yield bituminous coal of excellent quality for steam, coking, and for gas. Anthracite coal is found in British Columbia and in the Northwest Territories. The consumption of coal in Canada is about 5,000,000 tons per annum, of which our mines supply only 3,000,000 tons, the balance of 2,000,000 is imported.

A strange mineral, named albertite, was discovered at the Albert Mine, about the year 1850. It was regarded by some as a true coal, and by others as a variety of jet, and by others again, as related to asphaltum, because it resembles it in appearance, being very black, brittle, and lustrous, and destitute of structure. It differs from asphaltum in fusibility, and in its relation to solvents; it differs also from true coal in being of one quality throughout, and contains no trace of vegetable tissues; its mode of occurrence is that of a vein, and not that of a true bed. The mineral has been exported to the United States for the manufacture of oils and of gas; it is capable of yielding 100 gallons of crude oil per ton, and of 14,500 cubic feet of gas, of superior illuminating power, per ton.

COPPER.

Copper is stated to constitute one of the most important of the mineral treasures of the Dominion, and is said to be as widely distributed in nature as iron. It is found over vast tracts of country in Ontario, in the eastern townships of Quebec, in Nova Scotia, and British Columbia; traces of it are met with in New Brunswick. The richest producing section is along the northern shore of Lake Superior, where it frequently occurs in the form of native copper, in large masses. The next in importance are the deposits of the eastern townships, in Quebec. The copper ore here is similar in its structure and occurrence to those of Norway and Sweden, and is met with chiefly as a sulphurate in great abundance. The Geological Survey Report of 1866 enumerated the extraordinary number of 557 locations in the eastern townships. Companies were formed and mines were opened. Operations have been suspended by some, and others are working with varied results. Mining operations, of a somewhat extensive character, are in progress at Sydney, Cape Breton, where an assay made yielded 34 oz. of silver, 1-5 oz. of gold, and 20 ½ per cent. of copper, per ton of ore.

GOLD.

Gold is found in all the Provinces, except Prince Edward Island and New Brunswick. Gold mining is one of the principal sources of wealth of the Provinces of Nova Scotia and British Columbia. The gold fields of Nova Scotia are estimated to cover an area of from 6,000 to 7,000 square miles; they contain bands of gold-bearing rocks, with veins or leads varying in thickness from a fraction of an inch to several feet. Quartz mining has been carried on successfully, and gold, to the amount of $8,000,000, has been taken out in this Province, from the year 1859 up to and including 1885. All the gold produced in British Columbia has been from placer mines, which are worked along the banks and beds of the rivers and creeks at low water. The main auriferous belt runs from south east to northwest; the principal localities are Kootenay, Big Bend, Cariboo, Omineca and Cassiar, where at present there is considerable excitement in gold mining; they have yielded, during the above mentioned period of time, about $50,000,000; this should indicate that gold in immense quantities must exist up in the mountains; there are, however, differences of opinion about this. Several companies have lately been formed, with large capital, to carry on the business of quartz mining on an extensive scale. We learn from the latest reports that the prospects of success are not only sure, but exceedingly bright.

GRAPHITE.

Graphite is sometimes called plumbago or black-lead. These are misnomers, arising from the erroneous idea that lead enters into its composition. Graphite is recognized as a native form of carbon. Geologists are at variance concerning its probable origin. There are two distinct varieties: one is fine-grained and the other is foliated. Graphitiferous rocks of the Laurentian system are widely spread throughout Canada. The graphite of these rocks usually occurs in beds and seams, varying in thickness from a few inches to three feet. The analysis of the Canadian product is almost identical with that of Ceylon (the finest in the world). Its freeness from lime makes it very valuable for making crucibles. Canada contains an almost inexhaustible quantity, scattered throughout the Provinces of Nova Scotia, New Brunswick, Quebec, and Ontario. Very little has been done yet in working the mines.

GYPSUM.

The Provinces of Nova Scotia, New Brunswick and Ontario, and the Northwest Territories, yield gypsum of a very fine quality, particularly Nova Scotia, where it is found in connection with the lower carboniferous limestones. There are two kinds, white and blue, the former being best adapted for making plaster of Paris, and the latter for making land plaster for agricultural purposes. Considerable quantities are shipped to the United States, besides what is required for home consumption. 87,644 tons were exported from Nova Scotia to the United States in 1885, and an average of about 5,000 tons are shipped annually from the Grand River district, in Ontario, to the western part of the State of New York.

IRON.

Iron in unlimited quantities is found in all the Provinces and Territories of the Dominion; the country is pre-eminently rich in the ores of iron of every kind, and of the highest grade, equaling the Swedish and Russian in quality, and they are adapted for every purpose that iron and steel are used for. Nova Scotia is the richest in iron ores, and they are in close proximity to almost unlimited quantities of coal. New Brunswick has extensive deposits of iron ores in Carlton

County, and bog ores in Queens, Sunbury, Restigouche, and Northumberland counties. In the Province of Quebec, near the City of Ottawa, there is a hill of iron which has been estimated to contain 100,000,000 tons. The Haycock Mine is situated eight miles north-east of the city, and it has been estimated that it could yield an output of 100 tons of ore per day for 150 years, without being exhausted. Very valuable deposits of iron and bog ores are found in many other parts of the Province. The Province of Ontario has enormous deposits of iron ores of a superior quality; many rich beds have been found in Manitoba and in the Northwest Territories. British Columbia is exceedingly rich in iron ores; many of the deposits are found along the coast and islands, lying side by side with bituminous coal of good quality.

There is no other metal of so much importance to the material progress and prosperity of any country as iron, and when we consider the enormous amount we are importing, viz.: an average of $20,000,000 per annum since Confederation, making an aggregate for 20 years of $400,000,000, it is high time for us not only to consider, but to commence to make all the iron and steel goods we need. We possess 12,000 miles of railways and are increasing our mileage from year to year; these railroads would in themselves consume in large quantities, in addition to our requirements in other directions. Then, consider the bearing the iron industry would have on other industries, which would come into existence in connection with it; the benefits from it directly or indirectly would be incalculable. There are quite a number of chartered companies organized to work mines and to manufacture iron and steel who are waiting their opportunity to commence operations. A syndicate of wealthy and influential Americans, being satisfied that the Iron deposits of Canada are the richest in the world, and that they can be worked to advantage, have recently organized themselves into a company with a capital of $10,000,000, for the purpose of working iron mines in Canada. We wish them every success, and sincerely hope that they will be well rewarded; their movement in this direction may give courage for the investment of many millions more by others for the same and kindred purposes. The development of our coal and iron industries will do more to enrich our country than anything else we know of could do.

LEAD.

Galena or sulphite of lead is found in varying quantities in all the Provinces except Prince Edward Island. The counties of Frontenac and Hastings, in the Province of Ontario, are especially designated as a lead mining region, and the Frontenac Lead Mining Company is prepared now to carry on extensive operations north of Kingston. Lead mining, so far, has not been carried on to any extent, but it is expected to become one of considerable importance in the near future, as the facilities for transportation, which was the principal drawback in the past, have been very much improved by the building of railroads adjacent to many of the deposits. The uses of lead are so varied, and used in such large quantities in connection with the industrials arts, that the opening up and working of the mines would make this another very important industry of our country. It is only lately that it has become known that the Kootenay Country, in British Columbia, is enormously rich in lead ores, the ore showing as much as 15½oz. of silver to the ton. It cannot be mined to pay until a railway is built into that country to give them an outlet. I understand that a charter has been obtained for one, and that it will soon be built. When that is done, we may hear of results from there equaling if not surpassing those of Leadville and the Black Hills country.

MANGANESE.

The ores of manganese are found in all the Provinces except in British Columbia, and are mined to a considerable extent in Nova Scotia and in New Brunswick; their value is estimated on the percentage of binoxide which they contain. They are used extensively in manufacturing bleaching powders and flint glass, and as a siccative in paints, oils and varnishes.

MICA.

Mica is one of the characteristic minerals of the Laurentian rocks. In these rocks are found the white, brown and black varieties, of which the former is the most valuable. Workable deposits of the white mica are found from Labrador on the east, to Lake of the Woods on the west, whilst the Ottawa Valley is a huge storehouse of mica, in which the black predominates. Its use has been principally for lanterns and stoves on account of its transparency.

PETROLEUM.

This mineral product is also known as kerosene and coal oil. It has been noticed in all the Provinces except in Prince Edward Island. Its origin has been a subject of much speculation among geologists, and is still an unsettled question, the prevalent and most widely accepted notion is, that it is due to a very slow decomposition of organic remains, animal or vegetable, or both combined. The only area of production at present lies between Lake Erie and Lake Huron. The petroleum bearing region is overlaid with continuous beds of sand and clay, which sometimes hold the oil rising from the underlying limestones of the corniforous formation, which seems to be its true source.

Our petroleum oil industries employ a capital of $10,000,000; the production of the wells is about 6,000,000 barrels of crude oil per annum, which is manufactured into all kinds of illuminating and lubricating oils and greases, benzine, vaseline, paraffine wax, etc., etc.

There is considerable excitement existing at present in the neighborhood of Montreal, in consequence of the discovery of natural gas at Longue Pointe. A joint stock company has been formed for the purpose of prospecting in that neighborhood; they are at work now, and have drilled to a depth of 1,300 feet; the average daily progress is from ten to fifteen feet. The rapidity of the work, of course, depends upon the character of the resistance offered in boring down through the earth; they expect to find the gas at a depth of about 2,000 feet. There is an almost intolerable smell of gas coming from the shaft which they are sinking.

SALT.

This very important substance is found in the Provinces of Nova Scotia, Ontario, British Columbia, and in the Northwest Territories, but it is only prepared for commerce in Ontario.

It was first discovered at Goderich, by parties who were boring for petroleum, the boring resulted in the discovery of a bed of rock salt 30 feet thick at a depth of 964 feet; the boring was continued at a depth of 1,010 feet, when hard rock was met with. A pure saturated brine was obtained at this depth.

The principal wells are at Goderich, Clinton, Seaforth and Kincardine. The brine is of great strength, and of remarkable purity. American chemists, who have examined Canadian salt, unhesitatingly declare that it is of finer quality than that obtained from the great American salt area of New York State. Some distance up the Slave River in the Northwest Territories, a number of brine springs are found scattered over a wide plain, and large accumulations of salt are deposited around them. It is said that these accumulations are of unknown depth and extent, and it is supposed that there are vast deposits underneath the surface. Another salt region is reported to be at about half way between Great Slave and Great Bear Lakes, which takes about half a day to cross.

SILVER.

The ores of silver are found in all the Provinces, except in Prince Edward Island. There are, however, no workings to speak of, except those carried on along the northern shore of Lake Superior, including the famous Silver Islet Mine; the latter was originally a rock whose greatest diameter was 75 feet, and its greatest height above the lake was eight feet; it is situated about half a mile from the main-land. The vein was discovered in 1868, and was worked by the Montreal Mining Company for two years; they disposed of it, and 107,000 acres of mineral lands, to an American Company. Since then, the mine has been steadily worked, and extends now to a depth of over 550 feet below the level of the lake; it is yielding a remunerative return, and it is estimated that over $3,000,000 worth of Silver has been taken out of it since it was opened. The most remarkable discoveries of silver ore on record were made last March, in the Thunder Bay District, near Port Arthur. Mr. Roland, C. E., reported that the Beaver Mine has shown, by actual measurement, upwards of $750,000 worth of solid silver in sight, and that another bonanza has been struck at Silver Mountain, containing solid black silver in immense quantities. Such rich exposures of silver ores are unprecedented.

All the lead ores of the Province of Quebec contain silver yielding from 1½ oz. to 65 oz. to the ton; and all the lead ores found in Nova Scotia yield from 3 oz. to 100 oz. to the ton.

British Columbia seems from latest reports to be developing in minerals of every kind, and some of its showings indicate that it is going to excel in silver, and some of the assays made have shown as high as $600 to the ton of ore. The silver ores on Kootenay Lake, and on the Upper Columbia River, are very plentiful. There is every indication to lead to the belief that very rich silver mines will be opened there as soon as the means of transportation are completed.

As time will not permit us to enter into the particulars of all the minerals, I will merely say that we have in addition to those already mentioned, arsenic, bismuth, cobalt, lignite, molybdenum, nickel, pyrites, lithographic stone, oxides of iron of every kind, suitable for paint, materials for building, flagging, paving and slating; stone suitable for grindstones and millstones, marbles of various qualities, white, black, brown, gray-mottled, variegated, spotted and green ; white quartz and silicious sandstone, for making glass; soapstone, emery, infusorial earths, and precious stones. The early French settlers sent home considerable quantities of the latter, and one very handsome amethyst was divided into two and placed in the crown of one of the French kings. The precious stones are agates, amethysts, jasper, garnets, topaz, bloodstone and opal.

I have thus skimmed over an extensive area in minerals, but have scarcely touched on any points relating to them, except those that were necessary to impress you with the richness of their quality, the vastness of the deposits, and the wealth which they contain. Canada has unbounded resources in all kinds of minerals.

Let me call your attention for a moment before closing to a mechanical device called "The Cyclone Pulverizer," a machine which is destined to play a most important part in the reduction of minerals, which require to be either pulverized or fiberized; it can do either at much less cost, and to better advantage in every way, than any other machine yet invented, and especially is this the case in the reduction of gold quartz, mica, plumbago and phosphates, and in fiberizing asbestos. It has stood the severest tests on all kinds of materials which required to be pulverized or fiberized. A test was recently made on phosphates which contained a large percentage of mica, rendering it almost valueless for exportation. The mica was separated from the phosphates without any difficulty in the process of pulverization, and its analysis, which was only 30 per cent. phosphoric acid, equivalent to 66 per cent. phosphate of lime, was raised to 34½ per cent. phosphoric acid, equivalent to 75½ per cent. phosphate of lime. It is needless to say that such a showing will be of very great value to phosphate miners. Statements as interesting can be made in reference to tests made with it on other materials as well as on minerals.

232

John A. Fraser

"In the rocky bloom of canyons deep,
Screened by the stony ribs of mountains hoar,
Which steeped their snowy peaks in purging cloud."
— Mair

AN ARTIST'S EXPERIENCE IN THE CANADIAN ROCKIES.

BY
JOHN A. FRASER, R. C. A.   } *Read before the Canadian Club of New York.*

THAT I am very much pleased and gratified to meet this brilliant gathering of the members of the Club and their friends, no one can doubt.

I assure you, moreover, that it is very pleasant to recognize so many known and loved faces for "Auld Lang-Syne."

Most of you are aware that all the pictures here exhibited were painted on the spot. I mean by that that they were begun and finished, as far as you see them, out of doors and in view of the subjects or objects depicted. [*Referring here to his magnificent collection of paintings then on exhibition*].

And although, condescendingly judging from the results attained, it may seem to you to have been rather easy of accomplishment—and you will be surprised when told that like many another undertaking such as bridging the East River and digging a canal through the Isthmus of Suez, it was after all not so easy as it seems.

I may tell you that five artists, all "good and true men," were at work at the same time in these Canadian Rocky Mountains. I know one whose eyes wandered confusedly for many days, and whose hands hung helplessly in the presence of those peaks over which the clouds, with their ever-changing lights and shades, travelled ceaselessly. For many days, I say, wondering what to do and where to begin.

Some had brought mighty canvases which were eventually covered with nothing, while others were covered with a good deal too much. Some, when a subject impressed them as worthy of their brush, would commence it, but almost at the outset the effect would change, and the attempt would be abandoned for something else, which, oftener than otherwise, would result in the same uniform failure.

But there was one among us who, indeed, was a grand example of patient persistence. Although the smoke of eight hundred miles of forest fires completely hid from view every object more than fifty yards distant, it made no difference to him. He had begun his pictures under happier auspices and he faithfully repaired, day in and day out, to his chosen grounds, and "fired away."

That is one way of painting on the spot and from nature. Yes, quite a long way from her too!

I am no political economist, therefore I do not propose to tire you with anything about the exhaustless capabilities for development of this new country. I don't know anything about such matters; however, I have a sort of stupid theory, unprofessional you know, that the valley and delta of the Fraser River are alone capable of supporting a population as large as that of Great Britain.

I can only tell you in a disconnected way some of the things that impressed me as an artist.

I left Montreal on the 8th of June fully equipped to carry on my "plan of campaign." I had an abundance of painting material, almost enough to paint the Rocky Mountains from base to summit. I took a great deal with me because I knew I could not replenish my stock there. But I brought some of it back, and I have reason to believe that it would have been better if I hadn't used so much. You haven't seen all I did, you know.

I will spare you some of the details about the trip from Owen Sound to Port Arthur. We made it in one of the Company's splendid steamers plying across the inland ocean called Lake Superior. Soon after leaving Sault St. Marie we were for hours enveloped in fogs which alternated with rains; consequently, the scenery could not impress me, only when we came suddenly in sight of immense lumps of majestic ugliness called Thunder Cape and its compeer Pie

Island. I say lumps of majestic ugliness, for although nothing else but enormous basaltic spurs, they are majestic and imposing notwithstanding, as they rise from the waste of waters like *lions couchants.* At Port Arthur, with the words "All aboard!" the fun began.

We commenced to size up and sort our company, and choose our companions.

There was naturally a predominance of the Scotch Ontario element :—the man with the shrewd, rather suspicious gray eyes, not very grey, for he could not afford to let too much out ; eyes well set back under the square brow, the strong lines indicative of thrift, perseverance and strong settled " releegious opeenions "; the hard, stern mouth, and the fine well-pronounced freckles on the sole-leather skin, all of which characteristics proved him the honest farmer going West to "better his condeetion and tae mak muckle or mair for the wife and weans."

These thrifty Scotchmen kept pretty much to themselves, they did not " give themselves away."

Of course, the joyous, buoyant drummer was there in force, as he is everywhere, and I was greatly struck with the boundless wealth of the great Northwest, because most of those gentlemen represented houses interested in the manufacture of receptacles for the said wealth—their business in life being to sell safes; and, as they were very numerous, the inference that money was plenty in the Northwest was a fair one at that distance, although I must confess my disappointment on reaching Winnipeg, in not observing any more profuse prodigality there than in New York or Boston.

Of course, the people I have described, though charming

in their way, did not attract me very powerfully. But I soon found pleasant traveling companions in a gentleman and his wife from Baltimore; a Scotch gentleman from Glasgow, a right good fellow of a fine type, alert, intelligent and genial, though he did have the misfortune to be a "Laird," and a distinguished clergyman, also from Glasgow, who, twenty-five years ago, had been sent out as a missionary amongst the miners of Cariboo. He had built a church in Victoria, but had left it eighteen years since, and was returning to see old friends and scenes. All these people were like myself, making their first trip through to the Pacific.

And here, though she may never know of it, I must record the thankfulness of myself and friends to the brave and gentle lady of our party. I have not words to express my estimation of the uniform and unvarying kindliness, patience and sweet temper which she showed during the eight days of that journey, which was made in all sorts of cars known to men who deal in rolling stock—in box-cars, flat-cars, cabooses and cars of every description, except, of course, horse-cars; sometimes with no better sleeping accommodations than a cushion and a blanket. Our fare was *not* as varied as our transportation; sometimes we sat at table-d'hôte, in canvas hotels whose flamboyant signs bore such inscriptions as The Windsor, The Continental, The Brunswick, Grand Pacific, etc., where the menu consisted *always* of leather beefsteak well-covered with bad butter, boiled potatoes of the description known as "waxy," followed by pie, the whole washed down with boiled tea, and this without intermission.

Through the dust and heat, and clouds of bloodthirsty

mosquitoes when passing through the dry belt. Yes, through all the discomforts incidental to that first trip of three thousand miles, and up to the day that we left her in the fine hotel at Victoria, she was the same gentle, good and exceedingly beautiful lady. The love of those two people too was wonderful, inasmuch as they had been three years married.

You all know more about Winnipeg than I do, but here I want to acknowledge the royal manner in which Mr. Bedson, Mr. Scarth and the Manitoba Club entertained us.

We went with Mr. Bedson to see his herds of buffaloes at Stony Mountain and joined in the exciting chase—in a buggy. The hunt did not impress me as being as dangerous as it was uncomfortable, for three of us occupied but one seat. From Winnipeg our journey for eight hundred miles was quite uninteresting to me. The country, from my point of view, is wanting in the elements of the picturesque. When I say this I know that I am treading on delicate ground, for many of my brother artists hold that there is nothing so unpaintable as those subjects which, until recently, have been considered the richest in the pictorial element, and which are also considered as such by many whose names have at least the respectability of time and permanence.

But I am not sure that those among my brothers of the brush who have learnt to look at our glorious American scenery through the spectacles of France and Holland, might not find these eight hundred miles of prairies, coulees, and cut hills deeply interesting.

It was at Calgary, the lovely little town on the beautiful Bow River, that early on a summer's morning we got a first sight of the Rockies, fully one hundred and fifty miles away. The sky was clear overhead, and in the far distant horizon lay these mountains. Clouds they appeared to the untrained vision, and, indeed, as the eye gradually became able to distinguish and separate the forms, the poet's words,

> "The clouds like rocks and the rocks like clouds,"

was acknowledged as the best possible description.

From Calgary to the summit of the Rockies, on the eastern slope, is a panorama such as cannot be described in any way, either by pen or brush. For about one hundred miles it is constant, ever-growing and increasing in astonishment and surprise at its beauty and splendor. From the entrance of the Gap at Canmore, and up, up, ever up, past peak after peak, glaciers innumerable, over madly-roaring boiling torrents, toying with and playfully flinging here and there on their snowy crests, trees, some of them large enough to build a barn. Still up and up, until seven thousand feet above the sea level your train crawls past the base of Mount Stephen, its peak piercing the clouds a mile still higher up, and with head swimming and eyes and neck aching and your heart thumping against your ribs, you cry, enough! and prepare for the descent of the Kicking Horse Pass—and—dinner.

This pass of the Kicking Horse is, I am told, the steepest railway grade in the world, being four and a half feet in the hundred for about nine miles. I don't know whether this is so or not, but I do know that I was compelled to travel on foot and alone, weighted down with my painting materials and a heavy gun for some weeks, sometimes as much as ten or twelve miles a day, and in all sorts of weather, and doing my work besides.

Through the valley of the Kicking Horse, past the peaks of Lanchvill, a word or name which I am proud to say that I can pronounce properly, thanks to the persistent and continuous schooling of my friend "the Laird." It is a Gaelic word, and signifies the end of the valley. So, all's well that ends well!

Through this valley, amidst such magnificence of form and colors, on we go, till we begin to realize that one can have too much of a good thing. Presently, we commence to climb again, and the Rogers Pass, at the summit of the Selkirks, is reached. Here it was that my pride was hurt, that I realized how very little I knew.

We were heartily tired; in fact, we had reached the ultimate point of disgust at the regularity of the simple bill of fare.

Beefsteak is a popular and wholesome article of food; but beefsteak three times a day for many days, you can easily see must become monotonous.

We all grumbled, but a member of our party went off in search of variety. That town, up in the Alpine snows, was a curious and interesting sight. You tramped it from the cars over a path cut through many feet of snow, the remains of an avalanche which had some weeks before buried cars, shanties, tracks and everything else from sight. Subsequently I learnt that later on, in the summer, when the snows at this level were all melted, several freight cars were found still covered with snow in a little ravine sheltered from the sun.

Well! the seeker passed the grand hotels—few of which

exceeded twelve by twenty feet, and always constructed of tent cloth—till he saw an immense sign bearing the words " General Store." To the " General Store," which seemed completely hidden by the sign and a splendid specimen of Celtic manhood, the seeker hied, and addressed the large Celt thus: " Good Mr. Cap't, havn't you got a red herring and a nice loaf of bread, and some fair butter that a fel———" Here the seeker lost his self-possession, and his buoyancy received a rude shock, for the grand Celt, looking down with superb contempt, said in that rich, beautiful accent that some of us know and love: " A red herrin', at the top o' the roakies! Weel, weel, hadn't ye betther gang till the north pole and speer for plums."

I saw much of this grand Scotch-Canadian element, and wherever I met it, whether in the lumber shanties on the Columbia or Fraser, on the ranches in the dry belt, or in the warehouses, counting-rooms, or government offices on the Pacific Road, it was always the same as it is in this great country, where the Scotchman and the Scotch-Canadian man count among its best citizens, self-respecting, courageous, never blustering, honest and just, shrewd and faithful, cautious and kind, and always intelligent representatives. That was the sort of Scotchman I met wherever I went from Montreal to Vancouver's Island.

That is the kind of men who conceived and planned and built this great railroad. I am thankful that I have some Scotch blood in my veins, it may enable me to do something some day.

Oh, if my friend Eagan had only had a Scotch name!

I found the Pacific coast moist. It rained every day, and I

was told it was unusual; but when I looked at the purple and white bells of the fox-gloves growing on stalks six and seven feet high; at the gigantic bushes of the bonnie yellow broom; at the gowans at my feet; at the long ropes of moss festooning the mighty Douglas firs, and also at the rich mosses in the woods, three and four feet deep, I could not help thinking of my frequent experience as an angler. It has often occurred to me—has it not to any of you?—that upon arriving at a spot celebrated for its "immense strings," to be informed that this is not a very good time, last month was the right time, and about the middle of next month will be a good time. In fact, it has frequently happened that any time is better than the present. You can draw your own inferences, but fish!———

If the climate of the coast is damp, a very different story must be told of the country about one hundred miles east. Inland, along the valley of the Fraser, beginning at Lytton, where the dry belt commences, rain never falls. Still, by means of irrigation. using the melting snows from the mountains, it is a wonderfully fertile land.

I saw much that was beautiful in this part of the country, of a beauty that was new and strange,—golden brown hillsides and flat table-lands, benches so-called, and blue skies; but, owing to the fact that several hundreds of miles of forests were ablaze, the thick smoke prevented me doing much with my pencil. I remained there for some weeks and heard a great deal about the valuable gold washing, and mining, and cattle raising, and other industries peculiar to the region. Nobody there seems to think of doing manual labor but the despised and hated Chinaman, and he is there in strength; a patient, well-behaved, industrious, cleanly, sober laborer—and a very bad cook. That country could never have been developed without him.

I was much amused at a sign that I saw in Kamloops, which is about the driest part of the dry belt, the words were very suggestive: "Week Lung, labor done here."

I have said nothing yet about the salmon, which annually, millions upon millions, crowd and crush up the Fraser in their blind instinct to deposit their eggs. They know no obstacles, they never feed at this period, they only press on up the big river and out of it into the smaller tributaries.

When I reached Victoria, I wandered through the town with the minister, and we saw in a shop about a dozen very handsome salmon, the first we had seen.

I asked the price of the largest fish, that would weigh about thirty-five pounds. Of course, I meant the price per pound, as I would in an eastern market, and on being told four bits, fifty cents, thought it high, and said so. The fishmonger said he knew it was high, but the salmon had not yet begun to run; in a few days such fish would sell for two bits each. From which I gathered that fifty cents was the price of the fish in question—head, tail and all.

You all remember with pain the dreadful accident on the Brooklyn Bridge and its cause. You know that, in the procession, one or two people missed their footing descending the steps. Those behind them, in their impatience, pressed on, and the confusion increased. Those still further behind got anxious to know the cause of the delay, and pressed on. This was repeated still further back, and you know as a result that several poor creatures were killed, crushed and crowded even past recognition. Well, I am going to tell you the fish story. I have told it before, and my auditors as a rule have made no comment, but they have taken their hats, and departed rather more abruptly than politely.

I crossed a river walking upon salmon. Do you understand my reference to the Brooklyn Bridge catastrophe?

The advance guard of fish had become blocked in some way, and with just the same amount of senselessness—but what better could you expect of a poor fish—had choked the stream. They were all dead, and were jammed there in millions, for weeks, in many parts of the Fraser, which is a mighty turbulent muddy stream, fed by melting snows, and draining a vast area of forest land, one could not throw a pebble into the river without hitting a salmon; the water was literally full of them.

I stopped, when making the studies on the lower Fraser, with an Ontario family, who were not fish eaters; but I induced them to get some for me, and I enjoyed for several days some fine sturgeon.

I used to see these fish, weighing from two to sixteen hundred pounds, leaping many feet in the bright sunlight, clear of the river, in sport or in quest of prey. One evening, my host took me to see the sturgeon portions of which I had been eating, and much to my amazement I found it tethered, so to speak, by means of a stout rope to a wharf, the whole of one side had been cut away. He had begun to carve upon the other side, and the fish was alive and apparently doing very well. He couldn't have been happy, though?

While talking of fish, I was surprised at the presence of only a few trout in the glacier streams, and can only account for it by supposing that during the winter anchor-ice must freeze most of them. It cannot be that the water is normally too cold, as has been suggested, else why do we find any.

Referring again to the Scotchmen: at Donald, we, that is Minister "Laird" and myself, came across a philosopher. You will say that the heart of the Rockies is the last place in the world to find such a being, but there he was keeping a trackman's boarding-house. He had come from Cape Breton, and had early in life married a lass from Prince Edward Island. By a freak of fortune he had become heir to a large and valuable estate in Scotland. But, after having taken the necessary steps to secure it, he still hesitated at going to the old land to take possession. "Ye see," he said, "it will be a gude thing for the bairns, for they can be properly educated and take their proper poseetion becomingly; but for me, I've lived this rough life so long that the gran folks wad just laugh at me. Wull ye no hae a glass?"

Oh! that was a merry night we passed as his guests, Minister "Laird" and I. There was a violin virtuoso from the Shanty who supplied music for a very hearty reel, in which the "Laird" joined. A pawky lad from Cape Breton sang several songs in the Gaelic tongue, and an auld man with long gray hair took off his bonnet, and bowing to the Minister, sang in a voice to which tremulosity added sweetness, that gem of Burns', "The Banks and Braes o' Bonny Doon." He warbled the old love-song, sitting half in the gloom, the light of a common old-fashioned candle illuminating his beautiful silver locks like an aureole, while the night-wind sighed far up in the great pines and the mighty river roared in muffled tones.

God knows where the old man's memory travelled to, but we all felt the meaning of the song as we never felt it before. And we were the better for it.

Then, after singing "Auld Lang-Syne," the meeting came to a close, just the same as this paper does!

On the Bow River

246'

CANADA FIRST.

BY
REV. GEORGE GRANT, D. D.,
Principal Queen's University.

Read before the Canadian Club of New York.

HAT is meant by the phrase "Canada First?" It means that Canada—though still nominally and officially in the colonial position—is really a nation, and therefore that its interests and honor must be regarded by all true Canadians as first or supreme.

In 1867, the Act of Confederation constituted the Maritime Provinces and the old Upper Canada and Lower Canada into the new Dominion. Immediately thereafter societies sprung into existence in different centres that took the name of "Canada First." These societies did not last long. I do not know of one that is in existence at the present time. Their fate too has been held up as a proof that there is no national sentiment in Canada, and that Canada is not a nation. Is such a fact sufficient proof, or even the slightest proof of any such thing? Certainly not. It is only a proof that a club or society, if it is to exist, must have some definite object to accomplish. Any one may at any time be called upon to testify his affection or his loyalty or adherence to a creed, but here testifying becomes monotonous, and men will not meet regularly merely to cry "Yea, yea," or "Nay, nay." There are no Scotland First or Wales First or England First societies. In Ireland, there are societies enough to accomplish national work of some kind or another, but I have not heard of even Ireland First societies. The weakness inherent to political organizations that have no definite work to do is seen in the difficulty that has been found in forming and maintaining in existence branches of the Imperial Federation League. I am a member of that League, but it is evident that it will soon vanish into thin air, unless some scheme of commercial or political union is agreed upon, for the carrying of which its members may work.

Is there, then, a common national sentiment in Canada, independent of the vigorous Provincial contingent that we find in each Province? Is there a common life that binds these Provinces and Territories together? We have a political unity, but, does that represent any underlying sentiment? I believe that it does, though the national pulse is weak and is all but overpowered by the currents of Provincial interests, which faction uses in the most unscrupulous way, and by the cross currents of racial and religious prejudices, too often sedulously fostered for selfish purposes. This common life is made up of three elements: North-American, French and British. The atmosphere, the soil, the climate, and all the physical conditions under which a people lives, determine to a great extent its character and place in history. All these are North-American, and very far North at that. In the centre of the Dominion is the Province of Quebec, French to the core, French in language and in heart; nourishing, too, the sentiments, songs, laws and institutions of the 17th rather than of the 19th century. Then, Canada, as a whole, has inherited from Britain, not merely what the United States have inherited,—language, literature, laws, blood, religion and the fundamental principles of civil and religious liberty, that are at the basis of modern States, but also continuity of national life. That means a great deal. It includes the same traditions, the same political and constitutional forms; the same history, sentiments and affections; a common flag, a common allegiance, and a common citizenship. These things make up a great deal of our life. Every one knows how much the flag represents. And this Jubilee year will demonstrate the extent of the loyalty that all citizens feel towards the head of the whole Empire. We have undertaken to build up on this continent a Franco-British-North-American state, believing that these three elements can be fused into a common life; the experiment is being tried. Should there be success, Canada may be the link that shall unite the great mother and her greatest daughter, the United States of America. What prospect is there of the experiment succeeding? What proofs are there that the three elements are fusing or will fuse into a common Canadian national sentiment?

The formation of the Canadian Confederation showed that the people of the different Provinces had the national instinct. Autonomous Provinces are not willing to give up any portion of their power, even to constitute a nation. Any one will admit that, who knows the reluctancy of the thirteen colonies to surrender to the central authority the smallest portion of their independence. And, in our case, the geographical difficulties in the way of union seemed well nigh insuperable. To begin with, the Intercolonial Railroad had to be built along the St. Lawrence, involving a detour of two or three hundred otherwise unnecessary miles. Commerce demanded that the connection between Montreal and the maritime Provinces should be across the State of Maine, and the road by that direct line is now being built. So, too, commerce demanded that the connection between Montreal and the Northwest shore be by the Sault St. Marie and along the south of Lake Superior. And commerce made no demand for a railway across the Selkirks to the Pacific. But in all those cases, political necessities predominated, and the people have consented willingly to the enormous cost of building the Intercolonial and the Canadian Pacific railways as political roads. All that is now required to make the Dominion perfectly independent, by land and water, so far as means of communication from one part of the Dominion to another is concerned, is a canal on the Canadian side of Sault St. Marie; and its construction has been determined upon. The cost will not be excessive. There nature is on our side. If there was to be only one canal, it is quite clear to the most careless observer that it should be on the Canadian shore. The adoption of the National Policy, or the protection of our own manufactures against all other countries, Britain included, was a distinct declaration of commercial independence, that has been reaffirmed again and again by the people of Canada. The outburst of patriotic feeling, when the recent rebellion broke out in the Northwest, was still more significant. Though the French Canadians identified the cause of the rebels with their own nationality, or rather with the upholding of French influence in the Territories, regiments of Quebec militia marched to put the rebellion down. And patriotic feeling was not deeper in Ontario than it was in Nova Scotia, where various causes had combined to make Confederation unpopular. For twenty years, the Canadians have continued their resolute effort to accomplish complete national, political, commercial and national unity, in spite of the geographical and other difficulties in the way, that might well have appalled them. The present calm determination to protect our fisheries, and to waive no jot of our rights, although all our interests and feelings lie in the direction of unfettered commercial intercourse, and the preservation of friendly feelings with the United States, is another proof that we have become one people. The fisheries along the maritime shores do not directly concern Ontario; but the feeling there against surrender to anything like encroachment is as decided as in Nova Scotia. The symptoms of restlessness, on account of our position being merely colonial, and the discussion of plans, whereby we may emerge into a position of recognized nationality and stable political equilibrium, also shows that we are nearing that point in our history when we must assume the full responsibilities of nationhood, or abandon the experiment altogether.

I have said that there is such a thing as Canadian national sentiment, but the fact that the question can be asked, whether there is or not, proves how weak that sentiment must be. No one would ask such a question with regard to the United States or the smallest of European kingdoms or republics. Outsiders may think that it would be better for Belgium to be incorporated with France, or for Holland to cast in its lot with Germany; but in each case national sentiment is too unmistakable to make such a fate likely. Canada covers half a continent, and her great neighbor is certainly not as unscrupulous or as military a power as France or Germany. Yet, it would be inaccurate to say that she occupies as distinct and unanimous a position with regard to her future as Belgium or Holland. The fact must be admitted that Canadian patriotic sentiment is weak. Why is it so? Simply because we have had to do so little for the common weal. Our national sentiment has never been put to the test. Not once have we been called upon to choose between the nation and all that as individuals we hold dear. We have not been tried in the furnace, and the dross of selfishness is in us. Few of us have had to suffer, few of our children have had to die for the nation.

Far otherwise has it been with the United States. The thirteen colonies had to fight for their freedom to begin with. Rather than submit to infringement on their political liberty, they ventured to stand up against the disciplined soldiers of the mother country. It was a great resolve. It was a great thing to do. They succeeded, and so proved their right to be a nation. It has been said that they nearly failed. It has been proved over and over again that they would have failed, had it not been for this, that, or the other accident. The geese cackled, the ass brayed or the dog barked. But the mere cackling of geese never amounts to much. Depend upon it, there must be Roman hearts somewhere near, as well as geese, if anything is to be done. Even if the thirteen colonies had failed, failure could have been only temporary in the case of such a people. It has been said that Washington was not a perfect character, that his officers were jealous, his men intractable and mutinous, and Congress selfish and incompetent. But, supposing all these charges true, what has been proved? Simply that the hero is not a hero to his valet, and that an heroic epoch under mundane conditions is not wholly celestial. But, at a little distance, the picture is seen to better advantage. The mountain side is rough to the man who is climbing it, but to him who looks at it from a distant point of vantage, it is soft as velvet. It is seen under a haze, or rosy or purple light. So the events of the Revolutionary war became glorified to the generations following. They saw them through a golden haze, which concealed everything mean and petty. These events constituted an inexhaustible reservoir, from which the nation drank for nearly a century. Incidents of all kinds, love stories, tales of intrigue and danger, of desperate but successful valor were woven round every battle-field. The Revolutionary struggle made a deplorable schism in the English-speaking race, but at the same time it made a nation, and it taught the mother country a lesson that she has never forgotten. Nearly a century afterwards, just when people were becoming slightly tired of Fourth of July fire-cracker celebrations, a still greater thing was given to the American people to do. They were forced to choose between the life of the nation and an organized slave-power that boasted that the sources of national wealth were in its hands. They had to grapple with and strangle slavery or let the nation be cleft in twain. The choice was a hard one, but they chose well. It involved an expenditure so immense that no calculation of it can be made, but the investment was wise. There is no nation on earth so shrewd as regards all manners of investments as the American, and never did it make an investment so profitable. Literature and art, morals and religion, song, music, poetry and eloquence, all have flowed from it and will continue to flow from it for generations. These things are more precious than gold or anything that gold can buy. They are life. Sentiment and the almighty dollar came into conflict, and fortunately for the American people sentiment proved the mightier. No wonder that Abraham Lincoln's name has eclipsed that of George Washington. Who now dreams of dwelling on the petty skirmishes of the Revolutionary war? Every American citizen is now a better and richer man, because he shares in a grander national life. He feels its pulsations in his own veins, and he knows that his children and children's children will share in an inheritance beyond all price and that can never be taken from them.

Now, what has Canada done to show that she values national existence and national honor more than anything else? I have already gone over the record, and it must be admitted that more could not have been expected in the circumstances, and that there is promise and potency in it not unworthy of the stock from which we have sprung. We have no right to expect from man or nation more than the duty of the hour, and on the whole, Canada has not been unfaithful to that. Fortunately, or unfortunately, according to the point of view, we are not likely to be called upon to pass through the valley of tears and blood in order to obtain the crown of complete national freedom. On the one hand, it is perfectly clear that Great Britain will not repeat the mistake of the last century. In every conceivable way she has declared that our destiny is in our own hands. She gets nothing from us, yet she holds herself pledged to defend us, if necessary, against all comers and at all hazards. In making every commercial treaty, she gives us the option whether we shall be included in it or not. She facilitates our attempts to negotiate treaties for ourselves. She never discriminates against us or anybody else. Never, in the history of the world, has a mother country been so generous. We have imposed heavy duties upon her manufactures, utterly rejecting the doctrine of free trade, which to her is commercially the truth, the whole truth and nothing but the truth, that 19th century gospel, of which she considers herself the apostle to stiff-necked nations and colonies ; yet, she has uttered no word of official remonstrance. I believe that we may discriminate against her manufactures; may declare ourselves politically independent, or openly annex ourselves to the United States, without one shot being fired by her in protest. On the other hand, the United States are certain not to repeat the mistake of 1812-15. The armies that entered Canada then, to give us freedom, found the whole population determined not to be free ; at any rate not to accept the gift on that line. There is no more likelihood of Canada attacking the United States than there is of a boy attacking a full-grown man. And we are quite sure that the man has no intention of trying to murder the boy.

We are able to distinguish the bluster of individuals from the strong will of a great nation. We believe that, if a political party brought on a war of aggression against Canada, it would simply be performing the happy despatch for itself. We may protect our fisheries, and build canals and railroads where we like. The Gloucester fishermen may get angry and Billingsgate fisheries, and newspapers may solemnly warn the country that Canada is constructing forts, summoning gunboats from the vasty deep, and calling out her militia! Congress may pass retaliatory acts, and the President may even see it to be his duty to decree non-intercourse. But there will be no war.

The United States believe that they have enough on their hands already. A still larger number are convinced that the general well-being and the grand old cause will be served by there being two English-speaking States on this continent working out the problems of liberty under different forms. No doubt, many would like to see one flag from the gulf of Mexico to the Pole, but they know well that it would be better to wait for generations for such a consummation than to try to bring it about by force, or at the expense or the honor of either contracting party.

It appears, therefore, that our future will not be precipitated or determined for us from without. We must settle it for ourselves. And we are taking matters so coolly, that some think we have little interest in it, and are satisfied to drift or to remain indefinitely in the merely colonial position.

Charles Roberts, our most promising poet, represents Canada as standing among the nations

> "Unheeded, unadored, unhymned
> With unanointed brow."

and he asks reproachfully:

> "How long the ignoble sloth, how long
> The trust in greatness not thine own."

There is certainly nothing of the heroic in our national attitude. In his indignation, Roberts ranks us "with babes and slaves," and he seems to me to speak something like sober truth. A baby, when attacked, runs to its mother's apron-strings, and though the fault may be wholly its own, the responsibility is principally the mother's. When our newspapers hear of non-intercourse bills, they assure their readers that there is no danger; that Canada is bound up with the British Empire, and that the United States cannot discriminate between parts of an Empire, one and indivisible. When there is talk of the possibility of war, they hint of the havoc that British men-of-war could work on the undefended wealthy cities that lie along the Atlantic and Pacific coasts. But, let there be a proposal of Federation for the defence of common interests, and the same papers adopt a different strain. They point out that Britain needs her fleet for her own protection and the maintenance of her commercial supremacy, and that it is utopian—that is a favorite word—to expect that we should contribute towards making it efficient. Is not Roberts right? Is not that the baby's attitude? So, New Foundland is indignant at present with the mother country, because she was not ready to quarrel with

France for her sake. But not so very long ago, the same ancient colony paid no more attention to the strongly accentuated Imperial policy in favor of the confederation of all the British American colonies, than if that had been the policy of Russia, or a selfish scheme of the mother country that the children should consider only from the point of view of their own immediate interests. There has been too much of the baby attitude. We know what the mind of a slave is. He would like liberty, if it meant idleness coupled with the good things of Egypt. But Egypt to him is better than the desert, without food and water. To be stuffed with pork and beans, and to lie in bed or swing on a gate all day long, with nothing to pay and no master or no winter to come, is bliss unalloyed. When I read editorials reminding Canadians of the advantages of their present position—the protection of the mother country, no matter where they go or what they do, and not a cent to pay—I am reminded of Sambo's ideal of Paradise. Alas, if they only knew it; they are paying a price far greater than their fair share should be, according to any principle of computation!

If this is a true picture of our present position, is it any wonder that national sentiment is weak? What have we to be proud of? The wars of Champlain and Frontenac with the Iroquois; the raids into New York and Maine; the campaigns of 1812-15 have receded into the dim distance as completely as the wars of New England with the Indian Sachems, or the struggles of Virginia with the French for the Ohio. We Canadians have not been idle. We have subdued the forest; have built schools, colleges, churches, cities; and, as sons of those hardy

Norsemen, whose home was on the deep, have made ourselves the fifth maritime nation in the world. We own great ocean-going steam fleets, and have constructed canals and railroads as wonderful as any to be found on the planet. All this work, done most of it from "pure unvexed instinct of duty," is good. The man who has spent a lifetime clearing a hundred acres of solid brush on the wooded hillsides of Cape Breton, or along the shores of Erie or Huron, is of the same kin as the northern farmer who "stubb'd the Thornaby waste." From such an industrious, duty-doing stock, heroes are apt to spring. But the heroes must come, or we shall have only a community of beavers, not a nation. "We have something to be proud of," remarked a venerable gentleman to me not many years ago, "we have the best oarsman in the world, and my son owns a cow that gives thirty quarts of milk a day, and he has refused ten thousand dollars for her." Very good. We have not a word against Hanlan or the cow. But we cannot live on them.

What must be done? We must rise higher than the cow. We must make up our minds with regard to the future. Drifting is unworthy of grown men. Drifting means unbelief in ourselves, and abandonment to chance or to the momentary exigencies of party leaders. It means almost certain disaster. We must become a nation in reality, with all the responsibilities and privileges of nationhood. There are only three directions that can be taken, and the mind of the people has not yet laid hold of the question, with the determination to settle it, which is the right direction. We have before us: First, a closer political and commercial union with the mother colonies, and the rest of the Empire. This has been called Imperial

Federation, but it might also be termed Imperial Union or even Alliance. It would be satisfied in the meantime with a recognition of the right of the great self-governing colonies to be consulted on peace, war and treaties, and with an inter-Imperial tariff of discriminatory duties against all the rest of the world, as a means of raising a common Imperial revenue. Secondly, the proposal, made in whispers, of an independent Canadian Republic, formed with the consent of the mother country; and, Thirdly, the suggestion that the best way out of our debt and difficulties with the French-Canadians as well as with secessionism in Nova Scotia, and disallowance in the Northwest, would be by annexation to the United States. So far, the people have not seriously considered what should be done, or whether anything needs to be done, much less have they crystallized into parties on the subject. Consequently, not one of the three possible forms that we may assume has many representatives openly connected with it, although the conviction is deepening that any one of them would be better than the continuance of our present position for an indefinitely prolonged period.

Now, I am not going to argue for or against any of these possible issues. We are likely to evolve *peacefully*, in my opinion, into one or another. As long as revolution is avoided, the movements of nations are regular and in accordance with antecedent causes — prophet is he who can see into those antecedent causes so clearly that he can predict the outcome. I do not pretend to have this prophetic gift. The question is too complicated and too big for me. Notwithstanding all the light that has been vouchsafed to us by men who speak with somewhat of prophetic authority on the subject, the people still crave for more light. Any one of the changes, it is felt, will involve a great leap in the dark. Therefore, the man who attempts to argue for one or another should be a wise man; one who has meditated upon the subject in all its phases and who is not swayed by any selfish views; who combines a mastery of details with insight into principles; who is sensible of the gravity of the issues that are involved and who has estimated the cost for Canada of the position he takes; above all, who is too conversant with the difficulties connected with any solution to think that an epigram will settle it, or to insult by any kind of misrepresentations or rich name those who cannot see eye-to-eye with him.

All that I propose to do, in the conclusion of this paper, is to mention the stand-point from which I submit that we should argue the subject, and to consider briefly the recently proposed closer commercial relations between Canada and the United States.

1. Our stand-point should be that indicated in the title of this paper, of "Canada First." This means the settled conviction that Canada is not merely a string of Provinces, fortuitously strung together, but a single nationality; young, but with a life of its own; a colony in name, but with a national spirit, which though weak, is growing stronger daily; a country with a future and worthy of the loyalty of its sons. It means in the next place the settled conviction that the honor of Canada must always be maintained, no matter what the cost, and that Canadian interests are of first importance. Any man who is animated by these convictions is a true Canadian, no matter

what his views may be as to the political form that the Dominion is ultimately to assume.

It may be asked: How can Canada have at the same time the position of a nation and a colony? I answer that a country no more than an individual attains to complete self-realization at once; but, until it does so, it is allowed a place among the nations only by courtesy. As I have already hinted, the War of Independence was made much more difficult than it otherwise would have been, from the fact that each of the thirteen colonies thought itself supreme and the Union secondary. Even that war for bare life did not teach the lesson that a real Union was necessary to constitute a great State. It took some years of deadlocks before the present constitution was adopted. We can see how weak the bond that held the States together was felt to be—for a long time—even after that, we see it in the action of State Legislatures in 1812-15, justifying Great Britain and Canada, threatening secession and refusing quotas of troops; from subsequent attempts at nullification North and South; from political compromises and conflicts at various times: and, at last, from the great war of Secession, when thousands of men like Lee and Jackson, who cared nothing for slavery, fought for it rather than fight against their own native State. It took nearly a century for the great Republic to realize itself, to understand that its life was a sacred thing, and that whosoever or whatsoever stood in the way or interfered with its legitimate development must be swept out of the way. It accomplished the necessary task. Consequently its present proud position. It stands out before the world a power so mighty that we can hardly conceive of a force, internal or external, great enough to threaten it. Well, Canada stands now about where the United States stood a century ago. The circumstances are different, for though history repeats itself, it does not do so slavishly. We have had a different historical development. We have more radical racial diversities. We have a less genial climate, and larger breadths of land of which nothing can be made. But, we are near where the Republic stood a century ago. Canada is in its infancy and must expect infantile troubles. It must go through the hard experience of measles, teething, calf-fears and calf-love; must be expected to spend its pocket-money foolishly, suffer from explosions of temper, get slights that are hard to bear and abrasions of the skin that will make it think life not worth living. But, it is a big healthy child, comes of a good stock, has an enormously large farm, which is somewhat in need of fencing and cultivation, and I think it may be depended on to pull through. It is growing up under stern conditions, and, as a Scotch-Canadian, taught in his youth to revere Solomon and to believe therefore in the efficacy of the rod and the yoke for children, I am inclined to think that it is none the worse for that. The climate is most trying to tramps. Geography and treaties have united to make its material unification difficult. Much of its property is not worth stealing; but all the more will it hold on with grim tenacity to all that is worth anything.

But, no matter what may be said in its disparagement, it is a wide and goodly land, with manifold beauties of its own, with boundless resources, that are only beginning to be developed, and with room and verge for Empire. Each Province has attractions for its children. One would need to live in it to understand how strong these attractions are. Only when you live among the country people, do they reveal themselves. Strangers or tourists are not likely to have the faintest conception of their deepest feelings. Thus a man who lives in his study, or in a select coterie, or always in a city, may—no matter how great his ability—utterly misconceive the spirit of a Province or nation and the vigor of its life. It has been my lot to live for a time in almost every one of our Provinces, and to cross the whole dominion, again and again, from ocean to ocean, by steamer or canoe, by rail and buck-board, on horseback and on foot, and I have found, in the remotest settlements, a remarkable acquaintance with public questions and much soundness of judgment and feeling with regard to them; a high average purity of individual and family life, and a steady growth of national sentiment. I have sat with the blackened toilers in the coal mines of Pictou and Cape Breton, the darkness made visible by the little lamps hanging from their sooty foreheads; have worshipped with pious Highlanders in log-huts, in fertile glens and on hillsides, where the forest gives place slowly to the plough, and preached to assembled thousands, seated on grassy hillocks and prostrate trees; have fished and sailed with the hardy mariners, who find "every harbor, from Sable to Causeau, a home;" have ridden under the willows of Evangeline's country, and gazed from north and south mountain on a sea of apple-blossoms; have talked with gold miners, fishermen, farmers, merchants, students, and have learned to respect my fellow-countrymen and to sympathize with their Provincial life, and to see that it was not antagonistic but intended to be the handmaid to a true national life. Go there,

not altogether in the spirit of "Baddeck, and that sort of thing."
Pass from Annapolis Royal into the Bay of Fundy, and then
canoe up the rivers, shaded by the great trees of New Brunswick.
Live a while with the *habitants* of Quebec, admire their industry, frugality and courtesy; hear their carols and songs, that
blend the forgotten music of Normandy and Brittany with the
music of Canadian woods; music and song, as well as language
and religion, rooting in them devotion to " Our Language, our
Laws, our Institutions." Live in historic Quebec, and experience
the hospitality of Montreal. Pass through the Province of
Ontario, itself possessing the resources of a kingdom. Sail on
lakes great enough to be called seas, along rugged Laurentian
coasts, or take the new Northwest passage by land, that the Canadian Pacific has opened up from the upper Ottawa, through
a thousand miles once declared impracticable for railways, and
now yielding treasures of wood, and copper and silver, till you
come to that great prairie ocean, that sea of green and gold in
this month of May, whose billows extend for nigh another thousand miles to the Rocky Mountains, out of which great Provinces like Minnesota and Dakota will be carved in the immediate
future. And when you have reached the Pacific, and look back
over all the panorama that unrolls itself before your mental
vision, you will not doubt that the country is destined to have
a future. You will thank God that you belong to a generation
to whom the duty has been assigned of laying its foundations;
and knowing that the solidity of any construction is in proportion to the faith, the virtue and the self-sacrifice that has been
wrought into the foundation, you will pray that you for one
may not be found wanting.

This is our country, and this is a period in its history, the importance of which cannot be exaggerated. All of us, whether living at home or abroad, owe a duty to it, which we shall be base if we neglect. Confederation was a costly mistake, if we had not faith in its future ; a mistake that has cost hundreds of millions of dollars. But, so far as I know, the people do not think that any mistake was made. Every day, their national spirit is rising. We shall yet be proud of our country. In the meantime, let us all be united in heart, though we may not agree as to the best means of stimulating the purest patriotism. We may dispute whether a closer union with that wonderful Empire—of which we are a part - or separation, and the flying of a new flag, would be the better way. But one thing is clear; the question to be asked and satisfactorily answered, must be: What will be for the interest of the people of Canada? That includes, not merely their commercial interest, but the enrichment, purifying and uplifting of the national life. We cannot benefit the Empire by impoverishing ourselves. We cannot benefit humanity by doing wrong to our country.

The question of unrestricted commercial intercourse between the United States and Canada has been discussed at one or two meetings of this Club. It would not become me to take it up at this stage, save to say, that it too must be considered from the "Canada First" point of view. I am inclined to think that Canadians will say little about it until they have the terms of the proposed measure before them. The advantages of unrestricted access to our natural market are undoubted. Indeed, it seems to me simply impossible to doubt that the advantages would be equally great on both sides. We have always had the satisfaction of feeling that the fault has not been ours that the intercourse has been restricted. We have never terminated reciprocity treaties, though we have proved that we could get along without them. There is, besides, a standing offer on our statute book that has never been taken advantage of for the lowering of duties all round.

In the meantime, I trust that the liberal offer which Great Britain, with the consent of Canada, has made for a temporary adjustment of the fishery imbroglio will be accepted at once. Then, those possible complications that, under the present state of things, may arise at any moment, owing to the unauthorized action of individuals, will be averted, and the whole subject of our relations can be discussed calmly. No righteous man or woman in Britain, Canada or the United States, wishes any solution that is not fair and honorable. In this Jubilee year of our Queen, in a time when the power of the bonds that bind together the members of the English-speaking race is being felt all round the world, as it never was felt before, it would be an irretrievable calamity, a sin that posterity would never pardon, should there be a quarrel over fish.

2671

Awake my country! The hour is great with change. *Roberts*

THE ADVANTAGES OF COMMERCIAL UNION TO CANADA AND THE UNITED STATES.

BY
ERASTUS WIMAN.

{ *An address delivered at a reception to Lieut.-Gov. Robinson of Ontario.* }

THE question of Commercial Union between Canada and the United States is an exceedingly simple one. At the present moment, both countries have a high tariff, and a staff of custom-house officials along the border to enforce it. It is now proposed that there should be no tariff whatever between the United States and Canada, that there should be no custom-houses, and that the barriers that have hitherto prevented the freest intercourse between the two countries should be completely abolished. The proposition, while exceedingly simple in its statement, is freighted with consequences of the greatest import to both countries. It is of rare occurrence in the history of communities, for men to assemble and discuss a question of such magnitude as that of Commercial Union. It is difficult to conceive of a topic of deeper interest, or of wider range, than that which purports to change the economic relations of two countries so vast as the United States and Canada. Recalling great events in history, their importance is measured by the consequences that have resulted from them. The Crusades, the Reformation, the English Revolution, the withdrawal of the American Colonies, the French Revolution, the Napoleonic wars, all stand out in bold relief, because of the momentous consequences to mankind that resulted from them.

The American Revolution is probably, of all others, the event that has had the most direct and most important influence upon the English-speaking race.

In this New World, productive forces have worked out consequences which are almost beyond human computation. It seems as if, in the unfolding of the Providence of God, the discovery and development of America was the one thing needed to fulfill the destiny of His creature, man : for, without this discovery, mankind would never have reached his present material, intellectual and moral progress.

The growth of the forces that contribute to the world's freedom, to the easy sustentation of life, to the advancement of education and religion, has been immeasurably enhanced by the settlement of the English-speaking race on this continent.

It is not necessary to discuss whether this great development would have taken place had the allegiance of the American Colonies been maintained with Great Britain. Whatever opinion may be entertained on that point, the fact remains that up to this period, the United States have not only demonstrated the power of a government of the people, by the people, and for the people, but they have shown a degree of material progress far surpassing that of any other nation. Notwithstanding many and most serious drawbacks—of a struggle for self-preservation unparalleled in history—the progress of the United States in all that makes a nation great, rich, powerful and influential, challenges the admiration of the whole world.

Not alone does it challenge the admiration of the whole world, but it attracts emigration on a scale that has never yet been witnessed. This very year, people and their wealth are pouring into American ports. Skilled labor and inventors seek these shores, where Providence, in a most lavish manner, has endowed the land for the benefit of mankind.

The question of commercial union between Canada and the United States is of the utmost importance to the people of Canada, and they should rise to an adequate comprehension of its magnitude. It is not a matter of present politics, nor does it affect the principle of protection or of free-trade. It does not alone embrace the present condition of the whole country, but its future, and that of our children's children. Commercial union should not be approached in a dogmatic manner, or in a selfish and niggardly spirit. Conclusions should be reached only after careful consideration. To decide upon a question such as that of the enlargement of the international relations with a country so vast as the United States, is akin to a decision on the question of predestination, regarding which, as you well remember, Charles Lamb remarked : " That there was a good deal to be said on both sides."

While the world at large watches the progress of the United States with admiration, there is a general disposition to attribute their marvellous growth to the form of the government. While duly appreciating the natural advantages which the American Republic possesses for the working out of the problem of self-government on the grandest scale, the general disposition tends to attribute its material development to the genius of its people—because of their self-reliance, energy and hopefulness, qualities not necessarily resulting from a republican form of government. How much this has had to do with it will be found by a comparison with Canada, which, in the same period, under the wise and liberal rule of a monarchy, has also made substantial progress.

The United States, however, have one advantage over Canada, not of a political character, but which, if it could be secured by Canada, would insures her success beyond any question. This advantage consists in unrestricted commercial intercourse between the various States. The absence of custom-houses between them has done more to make the United States a great and prosperous nation than did the republican form of government. The arteries of commerce, in a greater degree than all else, have served to hold the people together, enriching them with the products and resources of each other.

With a different policy, a policy of isolation of the several States, there would have been no progress in the United

States such as the world has witnessed. Many of the States are poor and sterile, some are sandy deserts, while others can produce but one or two great staples. Yet, by a commercial union with each other, they have all developed material prosperity. Mankind in no quarter of the globe has greater cause to rejoice than the inhabitants of the poorest State in the great constellation of commonwealths. They rejoice in the fact that their commercial condition is so shaped as to enable them to participate, without let or hinderance, in the prosperity of the more favored States. Through the free interchange of the rich products of a vast continent, they all reap a benefit, and share in each other's prosperity.

With these facts before us, let us now consider what Canada has gained from her isolation from the rest of the continent. Under a different form of government, with a distinctive nationality, a commercial condition has prevailed between Canada and the United States, diametrically opposite to that which has obtained between the various States. Upon the whole, commercially speaking, the results have not been satisfactory to Canada. True she has made some progress; but this is in great part due to the frugality and energy of her people. It is true that her prosperity has been, at times, apparently as great as that of the neighboring States, but it is equally true that her progress has been spasmodic, and that her public debt, her provincial and municipal obligations, and, above all, the private indebtedness of her producers, have assumed alarming proportions. Of recent years an artificial prosperity has been imparted by means of increased taxation, followed by large expenditures for railway improvements that have developed vast regions of country. These outlays have mainly been well directed; they have, beyond doubt, brought within easy access stretches of territory hitherto so isolated as to be valueless. This apparent increase of the wealth of Canada, during the last ten years, from the doubling of railway facilities, is probably greater than that of any one State in the Union, but the price at which the investment is carried by the people of Canada may well be closely watched. If she can, by an enlarged market, higher prices, carry this investment without taxing too seriously the debt-paying power of her people, then these large public and private outlays will bear profitable fruit. But if the heavy load of debt and taxation, now weighing upon Canada, is to be borne in the face of declining prices, of a restricted market, and by an embarrassed agricultural community, it would have been better had such investments never been made.

Large investments in public works and railway improvements are justified only by proportionate increase in trade. No one thing would so much contribute to the increase of traffic as a complete interchange of products between the two countries. The building of the Canadian Pacific Railway is one of the greatest achievements of modern times, following as it does the constant extension of the Grand Trunk system. These two great arteries, with numerous other railways, give Canada means of communication of the greatest magnitude and importance, within her own territory, as well as with the United States.

The wonderful system of waterways with which nature has blessed the Dominion, has been made still more available by the expenditures of vast sums in order to connect them one with another. To-day, the Canadian farmer is paying the interest on these investments. No greater benefit could befall the Canadian tax payer than the stimulation of a trade which would thoroughly utilize these means of communication. A complete interchange of commodities between the United States and Canada, would more than anything else, contribute to that object. Any development within the Dominion itself would also stimulate traffic and increase railway tonnage. These advantages would certainly be largely enhanced by the removal of the barriers which now prevent Canadian commodities from reaching the United States markets. No one longing for the creation of a market could have planned one better suited for Canada than that of the neighboring Republic.

A long residence in New York and a daily contact with the people of the American nation, have imbued me with the belief that no others are so well prepared to become consumers of Canadian products. The country is rich beyond comparison: incomes have reached a point far above those of any other people in the world. There are more individuals in New York who have $10,000 a year, or $200 a week, to spend on their living than in any other city of the world. More are rolling in wealth in the cities of the East and the West than had ever been thought possible. American consumers are in a better financial condition and are more liberal in their expenditures than those of any other country. They want the best products of the soil, and no region is better calculated to furnish these than the Province of Ontario.

※　　※　　※　　※　　※　　※　　※　　※　　※

The discussion of commercial union has been the occasion for a great display of cheap patriotism. Patriotism, as I understand it, consists in the love of one's country for the furtherance of its best and dearest interests. True patriotism should not obstinately stand in the way of the country's best interests. Love of British institutions, of British connection, cannot be imperilled by a greater development of Canadian resources. No sentimental consideration should stand in the way of a policy which would benefit Canada.

It has been said that in order to arrive at unrestricted reciprocity with the United States, discrimination would have to be enforced against English goods, and that commercial union is but a step to annexation. These two objections are the two strongest arguments brought against the policy of freedom of trade on the North American continent. But when we think of the vast interests at stake, and how great, to the Dominion, the benefits that the measure would bring forth, the interests of the few manufacturers in Great Britain, likely to be affected by the measure, are as a drop in the bucket. It would well repay Canada to guarantee the profit which every exporter of British goods will ever make for the remainder of his life, rather than that there should be any impediment to a union, comercially speaking, between the two great countries of this continent. How many people do you suppose would be affected were Canada to admit American manufactures free, and still impose a duty on English goods? They certainly would not exceed a thousand in number. It is doubtful whether there are five hundred establishments in the whole of Great Britain that have a large interest in the exportation of their wares to Canada. From a close acquaintance with numerous English manufacturers, I believe that they would hail with delight any movement by which the Canadians would be benefitted. Better still, if it should happen that commercial union would so operate as to determine a reduction in the United States tariff—a very likely hypothesis—this alone would offset tenfold the disadvantages that Canada's discrimination against English goods might entail. In other words, the demand for British goods throughout the continent—if a lowering of the tariff of the two countries was to take place—would be far greater than under the existing highly protective policy which prevails against the goods of all nations, both in Canada and the United States.

All great changes are apt to inflict some wrong in a few isolated cases; but progress cannot be retarded by such consideration. A great railway often plays havoc with the symmetry of a farm, cutting it diagonally in two sometimes. The enforcement of a universal law affects many an interest, but that which achieves the greatest good to the greatest number is the standard by which all these matters should be regulated. Commercial union with the United States would confer the greatest amount of good upon the greatest number, therefore, it is difficult to consider with any seriousness the objections urged against it.

※　※　※　※　※　※　※　※　※

It is impossible to embody within a time-limited address all that ought or could be said upon this vast question. If a war were necessary to secure the great benefits that will be derived from commercial union, such a war would be justifiable. Has not England many a time spent millions of treasure and sacrificed thousands of lives for the accomplishment of an object far less important than would be complete freedom of trade on this continent? As to the advantages to be derived by the United States from commercial union it has been said that they would be far greater, from a financial point of view, than those which were secured by forcing the Southern States to remain in the Union; which, as we all know, was accomplished only through a vast expenditure of blood and treasure.

It has just dawned upon the minds of thinking people in the United States, that Canada was geographically a larger country than their own; and possessed the potentialities of a growth quite as complete as that of their own. It would redound to the benefit of the United States to aid these by every legitimate means. In a certain sense, Canada is a treasure-house from which can be drawn the commodities the United States need most, and which can be made in the highest degree contributory to her progress. If, as *Grip* in its last cartoon suggests, the genius of the age could sweep away the long line of custom-houses between the two countries, and, so far as trade is concerned, merge them into one, who can calculate the progress that would follow from such a change? With a great ready market, Canada would, within ten years, produce five times as much as she now yields. If her fields and farms were worked to their highest productive capacity; if her fisheries and her forests were made to yield the proportion to the commerce of the continent which their value bears to the total wealth of the world; if her mines, the giant power that is now asleep, awoke to the wealth-producing force which they possess; and if her manufacturers could shake off the fears which now encompass them, and meet the incoming tide of prosperity and seek the advantages of larger markets, what better prospects need one desire for Canada? Selling five or ten times more to the United States than she now does, American merchants in turn would enlarge their trade with the Dominion.

Of course, it will be ojected that if the Yankee manufacturer and merchant are let free into Canada they will crowd out the Canadian manufacturer and merchant. Well, all that need be said in reply is: that if the Canadians cannot hold their own when all the conditions are equal, they don't deserve the name of Canadians. It is the first time in the history of that country that such a disparaging assertion has been made. If the pluck and spirit which conquered Canada has deserted it, it is time we should introduce some new blood in the country.

The talk that any class of Canadians cannot hold their own against any other people on the face of the earth finds no echo in the minds of our fellow-countrymen who have already found a home in the United States. They experience no difficulty in holding their own, side by side, with the Yankees. As mechanics, skilled laborers, railroad men, or as occupants of positions of trust and responsibility, we find everywhere the native born Canadian. Always respected, always self-respecting, sometimes somewhat assertive, always self-reliant and abundantly able to hold his own in a fair field. Have we ever realized the enormous number of Canadains who have already sought the benefits of commercial union with the United States. It is doubtful if, in the history of any country—especially a young country—so large a proportion of the total population has, in so short a time, sought a home outside of it. The census shows the enormous increase of the Canadian element in the American Republic:

    Census of 1860—Canadians in United States, 249,970
    Census of 1870—   "   "   "   "   493,464
    Census of 1880—   "   "   "   "   717,157
    Census of 1885—(estimated) 950,000

It appears that to this date, fully one million of Canadians have taken up their abode in the United States. A million out of a population of five millions! What a tremendous proportion this is for a country which is making the most desperate efforts to attract immigration within her borders! Surely there is something wrong in all this, especially when we recall the enormous expenditures made, the heavy burdens imposed, to find the most promising portion of the population seeking a home and a future elsewhere. If commercial union did accomplish nothing better than to keep our young men at home, that of itself would be a great advantage.

Not a mother but dreads the day when her boy, her precious boy, will look with longing eyes across the border. What is the future on the farm for the little blue-eyed baby that looks up into its mother's face? If the little one is a boy he will at best inherit his father's fate. The mother knows how hard the father has had to work to earn a livelihood; she also knows what frugality must be practiced to enable them to leave the boy any patrimony. And the dear mother knows that while such a struggle for existence impends, the attractions across the border are forever tempting her beloved son from her side.

But, if the little one in her lap is a girl; if the clear blue eyes look inquiringly into the mother's anxious face, what fate does she read there? If her brothers and half the boys of the neighborhood are leaving the country, how hopeless is her life likely to be? The opportunities for a useful womanhood are lessened. The sweet love that brightens life may never come to her. The delicious odors of the new-mown hay, of the sweet-scented clover, of the forest flowers, may never be associated with that most joyous part of life, when love and betrothal throws a halo over all the world. The budding womanhood will wait in vain for the companionship that should complete her life's joys.

With that far-seeing vision which is innate to a mother's love, she cannot but take a deep interest in any measure calculated to keep her boys at home, in any measure that would secure the happiness and the future of the daughters of this promising land.

No greater calamity can happen to a community than the loss of its young men. The statesmanship that makes Canada less attractive to them than the neighboring country is a failure, no matter how brilliant it may be in other respects. Nothing would so much tend to keep young Canadians at home than unrestricted reciprocity with the United States.

"Free American markets for Canadian products would bring such a reward that contentment and prosperity would inevitably follow.

The Club House.

THE CANADIAN CLUB.

TO the enterprise and patriotism of the Canadians resident in New York belong the credit for having established a Club which to-day proudly rears its head among the great metropolitan social institutions, and whose fame has extended throughout the broad Dominion of Canada. It has become, under wise and liberal management, a great national institution for the furtherance of a more complete knowledge of the affairs of the Dominion and for the encouragement of her art, literature and commerce. It has knit together, in ties of closer friendship, the many Canadians who have found their home in the great metropolis of the United States. It has become the rendezvous of those of our countrymen who visit New York. It is the neutral ground whereon prominent statesmen of all shades of political complexion have discussed Canada's great future.

The Club was founded April 30th, 1885, and its first home was at No. 3 North Washington Square. It was formally opened on Dominion Day, upon which occasion its worthy President delivered a memorable speech from which I beg leave to make some extracts:

"When it was first suggested that a club, distinctively Canadian, should be formed in New York, there were some who felt that the attempt might not be attended with complete success, and that the objects which could be accomplished were both vague and uncertain. It was thought—inasmuch as there existed no organization of a similar kind in this city—that a combination of interests peculiarly Canadian would be a vain attempt. There was no Texas or Missouri Club, no Ohio or Pennsylvania Society; and, except the New England Society, which only dined together once a year, there was no organization distinctively geographical and having for its sole object the interests of residents in New York from any special section. Nevertheless, finding that there were about six thousand Canadians in New York, and that a very large proportion of these were almost unknown to each other, it was decided that a club which would bring them together, could not be but productive of most beneficial results, and that a mission of practical usefulness might be worked out of the idea, that would be helpful to all coming within its influence.

"Accordingly, a meeting of the Canadian residents in New York was called at the Hotel Brunswick. The attendance was surprisingly large, and representative in character. The first and subsequent meetings indicated an earnestness and enthusiasm which was a revelation to those who had originated the idea.

"It is clear to all who are familiar with the position of Canadians in this city, that they are *workers*. They come here with the avowed purpose of making a fortune, and of becoming useful residents of the great city that so heartily welcomes them.

* * * * * * * * *

"This organization has for its purpose the promotion of our common interests, the improvement of our social relations, the cultivation of a more intimate acquaintance with each other; in short, it is called to guide and direct those who hereafter may join us, in the pursuit of a career of usefulness.

"I would commit a great injustice, did I fail to recognize the hearty spirit of good-will with which, in this country, all efforts for efficient service are welcomed. The treatment of Canadians by Americans, so far as my observation extends, has been characterized by the greatest possible liberality and appreciation. The success of Canadians in the United States is the best evidence of it. Another indication of this prevailing sentiment is to be found in the words of encouragement which have been uttered by the press and leading men with whom we have come in contact.

"It is to be hoped that the Canadian Club will foster intimate intercourse between former residents of Canada and visiting Canadians as it will furnish an effective means of making them better acquainted with each other.

"It will unquestionably bring together men who would otherwise have proceeded in their respective paths without benefitting from an experience which is to be derived only by a closer acquaintance. Suggestions and ideas, which would otherwise have lain dormant, will be given shape and life. The formation of committees, whose special duties shall be to publish facts of material interest upon all matters of importance to Canada, together with a library of reference, will result in diffusing reliable information for the benefit of journalists in this country. Public men, members of Congress, or others who desire to intelligently discuss subjects relating to Canada, will find our Club the fountain-head of information.

✱ ✱ ✱ ✱ ✱ ✱ ✱ ✱ ✱

"The walls of this beautiful room, should be devoted, during the autumn months, to an exhibition of the works of Canadian artists. If Canadian art could but have a chance to impress itself favorably upon the wealthy picture buyers of this city, and the names of Canadian artists could be made as familiar in New York as they are in Toronto, Montreal and Ottawa, the Club would have achieved a purpose of the noblest and most beneficial kind.

"The pleasure which such an exhibition of Canadian art would afford Canadians, the gratification which the artists would experience in being thoroughly appreciated by their fellow countrymen in a foreign city, besides its refining influence ought to make the attempt worthy of the effort. There are other exhibitions of Canadian artistic skill which the Club might well encourage. They might take the form of collections from the Societies of Decorative Art, of woman's work, which, in Toronto and Montreal, have of late years been so successful.

The Reception Room.

Embroidery, fancy work, sketches, and all those delightful conceits of woman's leisure and woman's love, would exemplify the refinement, skill and taste of Canadian women.

"With time, still larger conceptions of the duties of

the Club, will suggest themselves. It is sufficient for me to say with what pleasurable anticipation we may look to an enjoyment of each other's society, and to the conviction that the usefulness of our lives, the completeness and faithfulness of our services, and the growth within us of all that is manly and best, will be promoted by such an association. Mutual forbearance, hearty appreciation, and a better knowledge of each other, may confidently be expected to result from the formation of the Canadian Club."

How fully the plans for the Club's usefulness, so well outlined by the President, have been realized, this book in part bears testimony.

The present home of the Canadian Club is at 12 East 29th Street.

The house is one of the few ornate buildings in this part of New York. Remodelled for the Saint Nicholas Club, which occupied it for the several years previous to its removal to Fifth Avenue, it was then leased to the Canadian Club for a term of years, and was completely overhauled and refurnished.

The Canadian Club has a membership of four hundred, which is steadily increasing. Its aims have been high, and probably, outside of the Lotos, no other club has given so brilliant a series of literary entertainments. Many distinguished American and Canadian men of letters and science have read papers from its rostrum. Its art exhibitions have been encouraged by the contributions of almost all prominent American and Canadian artists.

The Club is a great boon to Canadians visiting New York, and that they thoroughly enjoy and appreciate its benefits the large non-resident membership roll attests.

G. M. FAIRCHILD, Jr.

Elk's Head in the Club Hallway

www.ingramcontent.com/pod-product-compliance
Lightning Source LLC
Chambersburg PA
CBHW022020240426
43667CB00042B/1010